HARDENING, TEMPERING, AND HEAT TREATMENT

FOR HOME MACHINISTS

HARDENING, TEMPERING, AND HEAT TREATMENT

FOR HOME MACHINISTS

Workshop Practice Series

TUBAL CAIN

Fox Chapel Publishing

© 2025 by Tubal Cain and Fox Chapel Publishing Company, Inc.
First published in North America in 2025 by Tubal Cain and Fox Chapel Publishing Company, Inc. All rights reserved. No part of this publication may be reproduced, stored in a retrieval system or transmitted, in any form or by any means, electronic, mechanical, photocopying, recording or otherwise, without the prior written permission of the copyright holders.

Technical Editor: Bill Gilgore, Manufacturing Engineer

Shutterstock used: OSDG (front cover), warlord76 (inside front cover).

ISBN 978-1-4971-0521-8
Library of Congress Control Number: 2025933559

To learn more about the other great books from Fox Chapel Publishing, or to find a retailer near you, call toll-free at 800-457-9112 or visit us at www.FoxChapelPublishing.com. You can also send mail to:
Fox Chapel Publishing
903 Square Street
Mount Joy, PA 17552.

We are always looking for talented authors.
To submit an idea, please send a brief inquiry to acquisitions@foxchapelpublishing.com.

Printed in China

© Special Interest Model Books
An imprint of Fox Chapel Publishers International Ltd.
20-22 Wenlock Road
London
N1 7GU

www.foxchapelpublishing.co.uk

First published 2002
Text copyright 2025 Tubal Cain
Layout copyright 2025 Special Interest Model Books

ISBN 978-0-85242-837-5

Tubal Cain has asserted his right under the Copyright, Design and Patents Act 1988 to be identified as the author. All rights reserved. No part of this publication may be reproduced in any form, by print, photography, photocopying, microfilm, electronic file, online or other means without written permission from the publisher.

Printed and bound in China

Because working with furnaces and other materials inherently includes the risk of injury and damage, this book cannot guarantee that creating the projects in this book is safe for everyone. For this reason, this book is sold without warranties or guarantees of any kind, expressed or implied, and the publisher and the author disclaim any liability for any injuries, losses, or damages caused in any way by the content of this book or the reader's use of the tools needed to complete the projects presented here. The publisher and the author urge all readers to thoroughly review each project and to understand the use of all tools before beginning any project.

Contents

Chapter 1	Iron & Steel	7
Chapter 2	Principles of the Hardening Process	13
Chapter 3	Heating and Quenching in Practice	27
Chapter 4	Tempering	41
Chapter 5	Heating Equipment	51
Chapter 6	Casehardening	64
Chapter 7	Other Heat Treatment Processes	71
Chapter 8	The Measurement of Hardness	84
Chapter 9	Home Construction of Furnaces	90
Chapter 10	Safety Precautions	102
Appendix 1	Thermocouples and Pyrometers	107
Appendix 2	Carbon Steel Cutting Tools	113
Appendix 3	British Standard Steel Specification Numbers	115
Appendix 4	Hardness Conversions	117

Publisher's Note: This classic edition of *Hardening, Tempering, and Heat Treatment* is published as a historical reference and for informational purposes only. Many valuable insights can be gained from learning processes used in the past. However, these are not standard practices today and many may constitute a serious health or safety risk.

CHAPTER 1

Iron & Steel

If "Know your Enemy" is prudent counsel for the soldier, then equally so must be "Know your Materials" for the engineer – model or otherwise. Important enough when the materials are to be cut or formed, but even more so when we propose to alter their characteristics. And there can be few such alterations so extreme as when we convert a relatively soft and ductile material into one which is hard enough to act as a cutting tool. So, I make no excuse for this initial exploration of the nature of iron and steel. You can "skip" the chapter if you wish – it may be that it tells you nothing new, and could well seem to be irrelevant if all you want to do is to harden a scriber point! But to begin at the beginning is always a sound policy, and I hope you will bear with me; it won't take long!

Pure iron, known as FERRITE to the metals specialist, is a relatively soft material, with a tensile strength of about 24 tons/sq.in and very ductile. It can be drawn into fine wires and rolled into thin plates – about the only uses for it in practice these days. It is chemically very "active", combining readily with many other substances, so that metallic iron is seldom found in nature despite the fact that it is the most abundant of earthly materials. (The Earth's core is almost wholly iron.) The common ores are in the form of oxides, some, notably Haematite, almost 90% ferric oxide while others may contain as little as 25%, the remainder being lime or silica based stone. Other types of ore contain iron carbonates, and a very abundant source is Iron Pyrites basically iron sulfide and seldom used in the manufacture of iron directly.

Iron is extracted from the ore in a Blast Furnace – Fig. 1. Even in early times these were large structures, but today they are huge. The "hearth" at the bottom is 45 feet across and the stack 100 feet or more in height, with another 100 feet of "top hamper" above. A medium sized furnace will contain 50,000 cu. feet of material and will "make" 9000 tons/week: Fig 2. The largest furnace in this country is designed for 10,000 tons per *day,* and keeping it fed with raw materials is a major part of the plant operator's concern!

These raw materials are iron ore, coke (the fuel) and limestone to act as a "flux" so that the stony matter in the ore may be sufficiently fluid when melted. These materials, blended and sintered into a uniform size and composition, are fed in at the top. Preheated air is blown in at the bottom, through the "tuyeres", and this air forms by far the largest mass of material

Iron & Steel 7

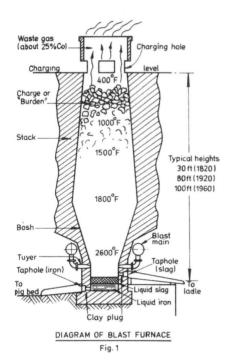

DIAGRAM OF BLAST FURNACE
Fig. 1

used. Though nominally "free" it has to be compressed to from 30 to 45 lb/sq.in, and heated to around 750°C, using turbocompressors of 10,000 HP or more, and enormous "stoves" to achieve the required temperature.

Combustion of the coke at the hearth results in a high temperature and the production of carbon dioxide. This latter reacts with the very hot coke and is reduced to carbon monoxide. This, in turn, reacts with the iron oxide in the ore to remove the oxygen content. When the gases reach the top of the furnace they will contain about 27% carbon monoxide, a little hydrogen, and the rest is carbon dioxide and nitrogen; it is a very useful fuel gas. By the time the "burden" reaches the lower part of the furnace the flux and stone will begin to combine to form a slag which melts and runs down through the coke. Slightly lower down the iron also melts. Both slag and iron collect in the hearth, with the slag floating on top. At periodic intervals the slag is tapped off through one hole and the iron from another, being collected in railroad ladles, the former being used for road metal or cement making and the iron either cast into "pigs" for the foundry or taken, molten, to the steelworks.

During the final part of this process the molten iron is in close contact with very hot coke and will absorb up to 4% of carbon. (This may not sound much until I tell you that a chunk of iron of 22 inch cube will contain as much carbon as a bag of coke!) The important thing to appreciate at this stage is that the iron and carbon form a *solution,* just like the sugar in your tea. After passing through a pasty stage while cooling the iron solidifies at about 1130°C, and we now have a *solid* solution of iron (Ferrite) and carbon, but with some of the carbon now combining to form an iron carbide. However, as the metal cools further its capacity to dissolve carbon diminishes, and some "free" carbon appears at the grain boundaries as graphite. The final state does depend somewhat on how fast

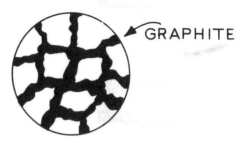

Fig. 3 Structure of gray cast iron, with flakes of graphite between the grains of metal.

the metal has cooled, but the "gray" cast iron which we use will appear under the microscope as small agglomerations (grains) or iron carbide and Ferrite crystals, surrounded by flakes of graphite. (Fig.3) If the cooling is rapid then more of the carbon will remain as carbide and the metal will be whiter and harder. Hence the occasional "hard spot" at the corner of a thin casting; the metal has cooled too fast.

Iron in this form is very useful; it can be cast into complex shapes and is very strong in compression. But it is less strong in tension and very brittle; it cannot be bent or forged. It is useless for edged tools and for many machine parts. Very early in the history of metals means were sought to render "iron" more ductile. These led to the manufacture of WROUGHT IRON, using a process which removed most of the carbon from the iron made in the blast-furnace. Pig-iron was melted in a coal or coke-fired furnace (Fig.4) lined with material containing a large amount of iron oxide. A certain amount of oxide was also charged with the pig-iron. About 4 cwt. was melted at each heat and when molten was, of course, in intimate contact with the oxides. The result was that the carbon in the iron combined with the oxygen in the oxides to form carbon dioxide – the reaction was very violent at times, with the metal appearing to "boil". The process was accelerated by the

Fig. 2 *Four medium-sized furnaces at the Frodingham works of the British Steel Corporation, Scunthorpe. These make nearly 40,000 tons of iron per week between them. The four hot-blast stoves serving the nearest furnace are on the left. The furnaces are about 220 feet overall height. (Photo, Courtesy British Steel Corporation).*

Iron & Steel 9

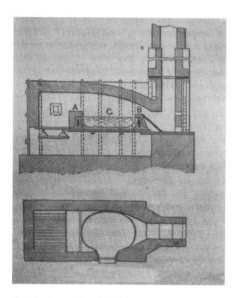

Fig. 4 Section and plan of a 19th century puddling furnace. The bath "C" would be about 6ft long and 4ft wide. The coal fire would be on the grate on the left.

furnaceman, who "rabbled" or stirred the bath with an iron bar suspended from a chain.

Now, the melting point of iron depends upon its carbon content, with pig melting at about 1130°C and pure iron at about 1500°C. As the carbon content fell, therefore, pasty masses appeared in the melt and these clung to the end of the puddler's rabble. When this "ball" was as large as he could handle he extracted it from the furnace and immediately set it under the tup of a mechanical hammer. (Fig.5a) The hammering drove out most of the slag in the ball and at the same time formed it into a bar. The process was repeated until all the iron had been extracted from the furnace, after which the furnace walls were fettled with fresh oxide on the lining and then recharged. About six heats could be worked in a normal 12-hour shift.

The bars from the hammer were cut into convenient lengths and bound together ("faggoted") with iron wire, and these bundles were then reheated to welding temperature and reforged into billets. This process could be repeated several times; each expelled more of the remaining slag and what was left was in the form of thin streaks.

The quality known as "Best" was metal which had been faggoted twice. "Best Best" was made from faggoted "Best" bars, and "Treble Best" from faggoted "Best Best". "Best" bars would have a tensile strength along the grain of the slag of about 23 tons/sq.in, while "Treble Best" might reach 28 ton/sq.in. The strength across the fibers would be about 15% less – the process cannot completely eliminate all the slag and this forms a fibrous structure within the material. Under the microscope the main body of the metal is almost pure Ferrite, interspersed with bands of slag, as seen in Fig. 5.

Wrought iron was too soft for use as a cutting tool, and from the earliest times a new material, having a carbon content midway between wrought iron and cast irons, was made from best quality faggoted bars. This was called STEEL, and any reference to metal of this name previous to about 1855 must be assumed to apply to this, and not to the "mild" steel we know today. The specially selected

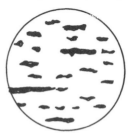

Fig. 5 Structure of wrought iron "along the grain" showing the slag inclusions.

bars (3 in. wide x ¾ in. thick) were heated in a box containing charcoal for periods of 8 to 10 days at a temperature of about 1000°C. During this time the iron absorbed carbon and as the bars were relatively thin this absorption penetrated right through. Means were provided for withdrawing a test-bar from time to time, thus giving a crude form of quality control. (Up to 15 tons at a time could be treated) The carbon content could be roughly controlled by the length of the heat, but if too short the penetration would be incomplete. Carbon content could never be below about 0.8%, but could easily be raised to 1.5% for (e.g.) the making of razors.

The process was called the "Cementation Process" and though it was effective the difficulty was that the carbon content varied from bar to bar and even along the length of a single bar. To overcome this, Benjamin Huntsman in 1744 found means of *melting* the bars after cementation. (It will be appreciated that to make a crucible which would stand up to the temperatures needed was very difficult at that time). Further, he used only pig-iron smelted using charcoal as a fuel, thus eliminating the impurities (phosphorus and sulfur) arising from coke fuel. After "cementing" the wrought iron in the usual way he melted broken up bars – about 50 lb. at a time – in special clay crucibles. This took about 5 hours. The contents of the crucible were then cast into preheated, split, cast-iron molds to form bars. Steel made by this process was – and is – known as "Crucible Steel" or "Cast Steel". By carefully selecting the intitial cemented bars – and, as a rule, using pieces from different bars made in different heats – very uniform quality could be achieved, far superior to the old so-called "blister steel". The cast bars could be forged, welded (with some care) to make larger pieces, or, for very large objects, several crucibles cast into one (sand) mold. The steel could, of course, be hardened (in the fashion later to be described – that's what this book is about!) but it was frequently used simply as a tough, strong material.

It may seem odd that we first make a material high in carbon, then remove most of it, and finally, add carbon to produce material of the required analysis, but a little reflection will show that as each step also refined the iron, to some extent removing impurities, and the final step introduced the carbon in the form it was needed, the process is not as illogical as it seems. The Huntsman crucible process was in use until very recently, and there may be a few small plants still operating. But the "cast steel" (or, to be more definite, high-carbon steel) of today is made mainly in electric furnaces, and the carbon added directly into the melt, with very sophisticated methods of analysis used to control the final quality.

The MILD STEEL we use today was originally regarded as a form of wrought iron made by direct removal of carbon, so avoiding the troublesome slag inclusions, and the intial patents of Henry Bessemer were for a "new way of making wrought iron". This he did by blowing air through a vessel charged with molten iron, and so burning out the carbon. Later, the open-hearth process, introduced by Thomas and Gilchrist about 1878, effected the conversion by the reaction between the molten bath and the furnace lining. Today, however, almost all mild or low carbon steel is made by blowing oxygen through a reaction vessel containing perhaps 300 tons of molten iron, brought directly from the blast furnace. Alloying elements are added (including the essential carbon) as required, but directly into the molten bath, rather than as in the cementation process.

Iron & Steel 11

SPECIAL STEELS – high alloy, stainless, and so on, are made by melting "mild" steel in an electric arc furnace and, again, adding the alloying elements to the bath. Whereas the first model engineers had but three ferrous materials available – cast iron, wrought iron and "steel" – today the choice is bewildering, and even cast iron may be had in dozens of grades and analyzes.

For our present purposes, however, we are concerned only with those which are ranked as "carbon tool steels". In general a "Mild" steel will contain from 0.05% up to 0.2% carbon and "Medium" carbon steel up to perhaps 0.6%. These last can be toughened by heat treatment, but not hardened sufficiently for cutting tools. "Carbon Tool Steel" will contain from 0.75% up to as much as 1.5% carbon. (Nowadays almost all steel will contain alloying elements, manganese especially, but it is the carbon content which determines the "nature".) Above about 1.7% carbon content the metal will be a "cast iron". A general distinction may also be found between "plain" carbon steel, which contains as a rule only carbon and a little manganese as alloying elements, and "alloy" carbon steels which will include nickel, chromium, and other elements such as vanadium and molybdenum as well as carbon. But all steels are basically alloys of carbon and Ferrite ("pure iron") and in many cases the presence of other alloying elements (especially in "plain" steels) does no more than modify the effect of the carbon. Even in the case of the "high speed" tool steels – alloys of iron, tungsten, cobalt and carbon – it is the presence of carbon which provides many of their properties. It is a salutary reflection that our enjoyment of model engineering depends entirely on the material found in the core of your lead pencil!

Fig. 5A Contemporary (1823) drawing of wrought iron being "Faggoted" under a water-powered hammer, with two interested spectators. (Copyright – Trustees of the Lonsdale Estate).

CHAPTER 2

Principles of the Hardening Process

Hardening high-carbon steel is easy – people have been doing it for thousands of years. Just heat the metal to cherry-red and quench in cold water and there it is – hard! However, like the horse (which is "... a noble animal but does not always do so ...") this does not always work, and a little knowledge of what goes on inside the metal will both make failure less likely, and also give some idea of what to do when the occasional awkward job appears. Those who find that horses *never* "do so" are always surprised how easy it seems when someone who knows about horses takes over! There is, they will say, nothing difficult about it – you just need to understand the animal. It is the same with steel. Nothing difficult unless you are actually making the stuff, and that part is done for us. You may have a slight problem with some of the "new words"; these I will explain as we go along, but you will also find a list at the end of the book to which you can refer if need be.

CRYSTALS AND GRAINS

When pure iron starts to solidify the atoms arrange themselves in a precise geometrical pattern, as shown in Fig.6. I have shown the atoms as little balls for clarity – we know that they don't look like that really, but we are not concerned with atomic theory, just with hardening steel. This arrangement is typical of newly solidified iron, and there will always be nine atoms, one at each corner of a cube and one in the center, at this temperature. It is called a "Body-centered cubic" crystal.

Such crystals appear here and there in the melt, and as new ones form they grow on those already there, the little groups growing larger until they meet their neighboring group. Where this meeting occurs there will be a discontinuity of the growth, so that when all is solid a look through the microscope will show gray areas with fine lines around them – Fig.7. (The crystals themselves are too small to be seen

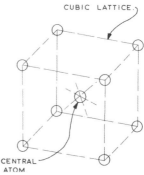

Fig. 6 *A Body-Centered cubic crystal of iron, with one atom at each corner and one at the center of the lattice.*

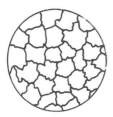

Fig. 7 *Structure of a pure metal. The crystals have "grown" one upon the other to form a mosaic of "grains".*

through an ordinary microscope). These areas are the "grains". As a rule, the smaller the grains (within reason) the better, and part of the job of heat treatment is to "refine" the metal to reduce grain size. Pure iron (Ferrite) tends to form large grains.

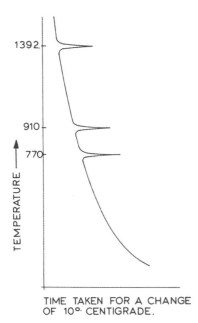

TIME TAKEN FOR A CHANGE OF 10° CENTIGRADE.

Fig. 8 *The cooling curve of pure iron, showing the three "arrest points" where the rate of temperature change slows down.*

The metal now cools still further, and when we reach 1392°C an odd thing happens. The fall in temperature is arrested for a short while, almost as if there is a source of heat within the metal. (Fig.8.) This is, in fact, the case, for there is a change taking place in the crystal structure which actually releases heat. (Metallurgists call this an "arrest point" in the cooling of the metal). If you

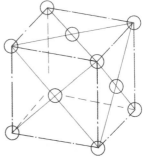

Fig. 9 *A Face-Centered Cubic crystal, with one atom of each corner and one in the center of each face of the lattice. (Those at the back have been left out for clarity).*

had suitable equipment you would see the crystals rearranging themselves, actually disintegrating and reforming in a new pattern. It is still "cubic", but this time with an atom in each corner and one in the center of each face, 14 in all – Fig. 9. This is called a "FACE-centered cubic" crystal. Again, these crystals form aggregates which meet at the grain boundaries. That such a change is possible may seem surprising, for though the metal is pretty hot it *is* a solid, and you would have to hit it fairly sharply with a hammer to change its shape. Things would seem very different if you were one of the atoms! Even at workshop temperature there would be some distance between you and the next one and at this high temperature you would find you had plenty of room. What appears to us as a "solid" is, in fact,

14   HARDENING, TEMPERING, AND HEAT TREATMENT FOR HOME MACHINISTS

mostly empty space, even within the crystal; it is the forces which act between the atoms which give us the sensation of solidity.

Not only that. The atoms themselves don't stand still. True, they cannot chase about as they do in a liquid or a gas, but they *do* vibrate about their mean position. (In fact, it is this vibration which generates the colored light we associate with hot metal). In such circumstances it is not so surprising that some of the atoms can drift about a little. They do this all the time at high temperatures, and at this "critical" temperature they carry out a complete rearrangement.

As the metal cools further we meet yet another "arrest point", this time at 910°C. This heralds a change back to the original Body-centered cubic shape of Fig.6. This is the "bright red" and about the temperature we should normally use for forging. Cooling down still further there is found an arrest point again, at 770°C. There is no change of crystal structure here, but this is the point at which the metal can become magnetic. (It is sometimes called the "Curie" point). This change in magnetic properties can be a useful indicator of temperature for some purposes.

All of these changes occur in reverse order when the metal is heated, but at the arrest points the metal seems to "hang back" and not get any hotter for a short while. Again, this can be a useful temperature indication. It is important, however, to observe that we have been talking of a *gradual* temperature change. Though the atoms are relatively mobile when hot they "drift" or "diffuse" rather than "travel". The changes all take time to complete. The presence of other elements – impurities, or alloying material – can sometimes make the metamorphosis slower still. Finally, the actual temperature at which the arrest points occur is very slightly different when heating from that found when cooling.

EFFECT OF CARBON

The presence of carbon has a marked effect on the behavior of the metal. When molten, the carbon is dissolved in the iron, as we saw in the last chapter – it is the same for molten steel as for cast iron. One immediate effect is to lower the point at which solidification starts and, in addition, to spread the solidification process over a temperature *range.* The magnitude of this depression and the range of solidification temperatures depends on the amount of carbon present but in the case of (say) a 0.5% carbon steel the initial solidification point (the "liquidus") is lowered to about 1500°C – about 50°C below that of pure iron – and the "solidus", when all is solid, is not reached until 1430°C. In between these two temperatures the metal is pasty, metal crystals and molten metal being present together. (You will have found the same thing with some grades of solder). Now, the carbon and iron are in solution when liquid, and this state prevails when solid as well. I have mentioned this in Ch.I "in passing" and it does need some explanation.

If the iron and carbon were a *mixture* we should have measurable particles of the two substances uniformly distributed. They might, however, separate out, as when the pigment in paint settles in the bottom of a can. No matter how finely ground, these particles each contain thousands of millions of atoms. A "solution" is very different. Here we have the individual *atoms* forming the dispersion. The scale is very different. It is feasible – indeed, normal – to find such an atomic dispersion ("solution") in a

Principles of the Hardening Process   15

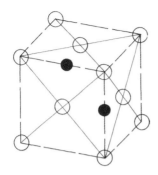

Fig. 10 *Crystal of a solid solution of carbon in iron, the small carbon atoms lodged in the empty spaces in the lattice.*

solid – a well-made ice pop is an example.

The carbon atoms are found actually within the Ferrite crystals (they are much smaller than the Ferrite atoms) as shown in Fig. 10. The number of dissolved atoms which can be accommodated in this way does depend on the temperature (as in the case of any liquid solution) but it also depends on the type of crystal, too. (This has an important bearing on the hardening process, as we will see later). Further, although they are situated within the crystal lattice the carbon atoms can drift or diffuse just as can the atoms of iron, but this drift can occur at any time, not just at the arrest temperatures. We will see later that the iron and carbon atoms can also be present in the form of a "Compound" – iron carbide – but this need not concern us at the moment.

To return to our newly solidified metal, the first effect of the carbon has been to depress the melting point and to cause a pasty stage during solidification. Once solid, the carbon is found in solid solution. In addition, however, the presence of carbon inhibits the first crystal form found in pure iron. The metal solidifies directly into the Face-center cubic form of Fig 9, but with many of the crystal atoms containing carbon atoms, as shown in Fig 10. There is NO arrest point at 1392°C. This "Solid Solution", with face-centered crystals, is called "AUSTENITE", after the metallurgist Sir William Austen, who first identified it. Grains of crystals are found, as in the case of pure iron.

Still following our 0.5% carbon steel as it cools we find an arrest point at about 780°C, where the crystal structure changes to Body-centered cubic – you will see that this occurs about 120°C lower than in the case of pure iron. The magnetic change, or "Curie Point" takes place a few degrees lower (about 770°C).

Thus, the immediate effect of no more than 0.5% carbon has been, first, to depress the melting point and to introduce a pasty stage in the solidification, to eliminate altogether one of the arrest points and its associated crystal metamorphosis, and to reduce the temperature at which the others occur. This may not, at first, seem to be of great importance, but it is the implications of these changes which matter, and they have a profound effect on the heat treatment. You *cannot* harden pure iron, but even 0.5% carbon steel can be toughened, even if not made hard enough to use as a cutting tool.

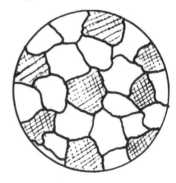

Fig. 11 *Austenite (shaded) surrounded by grains of Ferrite.*

IRON-CARBON TRANSFORMATIONS

Let us now follow this 0.5% carbon steel as it cools, but with more attention to what is happening to the carbon and the Ferrite this time. At solidification the Austenite is a homogeneous solution of both substances. However, as soon as the steel passes the arrest point at about 780°C and cools further, the composition of the Austenite slowly changes, until at about 735°C it contains 0.83% carbon – the maximum it can hold at this temperature. It can only achieve this enrichment of carbon by ejecting Ferrite atoms, and this it does progressively as the temperature falls. (The steel only contained 0.5% carbon to start with). This Ferrite forms grains or bands surrounding the grains of Austenite, which now form only part of the whole. The overall analysis of the steel will still show 0.5% of carbon, but it is all concentrated in the Austenite grains. Fig. 11.

Just below this temperature, at 730°C, we find another "arrest point", this time due to a change in the relationship of the carbon and Ferrite in the Austenite. Above 735°C the carbon is in solution, but at 730°C it actually *combines* with some of the iron to form *Iron Carbide*. This is FE_3C, and contains about 6.7% carbon. It is very hard indeed and is given the name "CEMENTITE", because it was first identified in steel made by the Cementation process – see page 11.

This Cementite contains much less Ferrite (iron) than the Austenite from which it was formed, so that there will be some Ferrite left over. In the event, the Cementite (or iron carbide) crystallizes into very thin plates, with similar thin plates of Ferrite sandwiched between them, this assembly of plates forming a "grain" corresponding with the grain

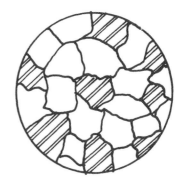

Fig. 12 *The Austenite of Fig. 11 has transformed to Pearlite, but the Ferrite remains unchanged. There is some alteration in the disposition of the grains.*

of Austenite from which it came. Under the microscope these grains have a very beautiful sheen, resembling that of Mother-of-Pearl. For this reason it is called "PEARLITE". (I am sorry about all these names, but there is a glossary at the end of the book if you find them difficult to remember). The overall composition of Pearlite is 0.83% carbon still, so that as the steel contains only 0.5% we should expect the Pearlite grains to be surrounded by grains of Ferrite, and this is, in fact the case. See Fig 12.

This recombination of Austenite into Pearlite occurs in *all* carbon steel when cooled slowly. Naturally, the amount of Pearlite will depend on the carbon content initially, but it is always there in greater or less proportion. Being a combination of soft and ductile iron (Ferrite) and very hard Cementite, it is very tough.

THE IRON-CARBON DIAGRAM

If we were to look at steel with a different carbon content we should find similar changes taking place, but at *different temperatures*. For convenience, engineers and metallurgists assemble the data on a chart, called the "Iron-Carbon Equilibrium

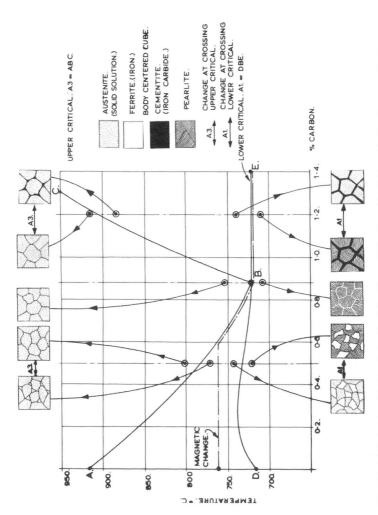

Fig. 13 A simplified version of the "Iron-Carbon Equilibrium Diagram." (After "Quenching Fluids and the Heat Treatment of Steel" Courtesy BP Ltd).

18 HARDENING, TEMPERING, AND HEAT TREATMENT FOR HOME MACHINISTS

Diagram", which shows the effects of both carbon and temperature. I have made a simplified version of this in Fig 13; this deals only with "steel" (the full diagram includes cast iron as well) and I have not bothered with the temperatures up in the melting range. Those sufficiently interested will find the complete diagram in most books on the Metallurgy of Steel, but there is a very clear one in Encyclopedia Britannica, in the section headed "Iron and Steel". This can be looked at in most public libraries.

I have shown the 0.5% steel we have just considered as a vertical line. The upper arrest point, or critical temperature, is shown by the line ABE, and the lower by DBE. You will notice that these coincide at "B"; we will have a look at this in a moment, but before doing so, let us look at a typical tool-steel, with a carbon content of (say) 1.2%. I have shown a vertical line here also. We start with Austenite as before, but this time it contains *more* than the 0.83% which is the maximum which can be held in solution at the lower critical temperature. (This is about 720°C in this case). As the steel cools below the upper critical, which is at about 900°C, the Austenite finds itself too rich in *carbon* this time, whereas the previous example was rich in Ferrite. So, as the temperature falls carbon is progressively rejected, but it is rejected in the form of *iron carbide* (Cementite) for, unlike the case of cast iron, free carbon cannot exist under these conditions. We find, therefore, that the grains of Austenite are now being surrounded by first, streaks, and then grains, of Cementite; there is *no* free Ferrite available. By the time the steel has reached the lower critical temperature (the line BE) the Austenite has again settled down with 0.83% dissolved carbon, as before. And, as before, this transforms to Pearlite as

Fig. 14 *Grains of Pearlite surrounded by borders of Iron Carbide (Cementite).*

the metal cools through the critical. We now find grains of Pearlite surrounded by areas of Cementite, (Fig. 14) in contrast to the Pearlite and Ferrite of the lower carbon steel.

Now look at steel with 0.83% carbon. You will notice that the two lines representing the upper and lower critical temperatures (the "arrest points") now coincide. It is, after a fashion, a "Eutectic" solution, similar to that found in solders and brazing alloys. Both the crystal transformation and the metamorphosis of the Austenite occur at the same time, and the Austenite changes to Pearlite directly. This "all Pearlite" steel is about the toughest that can be had with a plain carbon steel. You will note that as a consequence of this "Eutectoid" at 0.83% carbon the upper critical temperatures for the various steels vary considerably, along the line ABE. This has an important bearing on the temperatures needed to effect the annealing of the steel. The lower critical temperature, DBE, does vary a little, but in many published versions of the diagram it is shown as a straight line. The difference is only a few degrees.

I have shown on the diagram a number of little sketches indicating the grain formation – actual micrographs would be

Principles of the Hardening Process 19

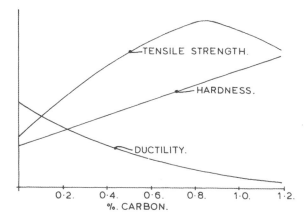

Fig. 15 *The effect of carbon content on the mechanical properties of annealed steel.*

confusing and are difficult to reproduce. However, by examining a specimen through the microscope an experienced metallurgist can easily recognize the various constituents of Pearlite, Ferrite, and Cementite, and by noting the proportions of each can make a fair estimate of the overall carbon content of the specimen.

To sum up: we would expect to find very little Pearlite and a lot of Ferrite in a low carbon (mild) steel, with the proportion of Pearlite increasing as we approach 0.83% carbon. Beyond this the Cementite would begin to appear, increasing in proportion as the carbon content rose to the maximum associated with a "steel" (about 1.7% carbon). We would expect the "toughness" and strength to increase as the Pearlite proportion increased, up to 0.83% carbon. Thereafter the steel could be expected to get harder, with some loss of ductility. This is, in fact, the case. Fig 15. But I must emphasize that these considerations all apply *only* to steel which has been both heated and cooled SLOWLY, so that the little atoms have time to find their right places, and the chemical changes at the lower critical line have time to complete. It is typical of a "hot rolled bar" which has (or should have) been normalized when you receive it from the merchant. Cold drawing (e.g. "Bright Drawn Mild Steel") will not alter the *type* of structure (Pearlite-Ferrite, or Pearlite-Cementite) though it may alter the mechanical strength, and especially the ductility, because the forming process has distorted the grains. The structures found when the steel is cooled too quickly for the changes to occur are very different. So, let us now have a look at the effect of other than slow cooling.

EFFECT OF COOLING RATE

Let us again consider our piece of 1.2% carbon steel at (say) 800°C, which temperature has been reached either by slow cooling or slow heating. The Austenite will have partly transformed, and there will be Austenite grains surrounded by some Cementite. Within the Austenite most of the crystals will contain one or more carbon atoms – the "solid solution" condition. Now let us reduce the temperature very quickly. There will be no time for the atoms to rearrange themselves, no time for crystal transformation, and instead of finding themselves in a lattice formation which leaves them plenty of room the carbon atoms are trapped inside the crystals with inadequate space for them. In addition, the Austenite is compelled to retain far more carbon that it can normally hold at the lower temperature. The Austenite crystals are put under enormous internal stress, and this is just the condition which is associated with hardness. In addition, the Cementite which is present is unable to crystalize normally, but instead is constrained into a needle-like structure (known as an "Acicular" formation) which is very hard indeed. In fact, it is these "needles" which help in the formation of a good cutting edge. This new structure – highly stressed crystals associated with acicular crystals of Cementite – is given the name MARTENSITE, and is the basis of all hardened carbon steel.

I have already referred to the need to *heat* the metal slowly, partly to ensure that the various transformations have time to occur, but this is also necessary so that we can be sure that the metal is hot *right through.* It does take time for the heat to travel through to the interior. A similar consideration applies when cooling. When cooling rapidly ("quenching") what about the metal in the middle of the workpiece? The outside has cooled fast, it is true, but it is clear that (with large specimens especially) the core may not have kept up with the cooling of the exterior. What is the effect on the metal? We can best answer this question with another diagram, Fig. 16. This shows temperature on the vertical scale, and time on the horizontal. Because metallurgists and engineers need to examine cooling rates which may last hours or days as well as those which take only the odd second or so the time scale is compressed – it is, in fact "logarithmic". The diagram

shown relates to no particular steel, but it is typical of most; every steel specification has its own "S-curve" like this. It is important to realize that, so far as we are concerned, it must be used only to *illustrate* the effects of time/temperature changes. Detail interpretation of the diagram is a matter for experts.

Looking at Fig. 16 you will see that there are two "S" shaped curves. On the left of the line ABC we have a zone where the steel is Austenitic (in a state of solid solution) but it is "unstable" – it has not yet transformed but is ready to do so. On the right of the line DEF we have the steel in its final, totally transformed state. In this area, if we were talking about the 1.2% carbon steel there would be grains of Pearlite surrounded by Cementite; if it were the 0.5% steel we looked at earlier there would be grains of Pearlite surrounded by Ferrite. In between the two "S" curves the structure is undergoing the transformation process and will consist of a mixture of Cementite (carbides), Pearlite and Ferrite and, of course, some of the original Austenite – carbon in solid solution. The nearer to the line ABC, the more Austenite, while close to the line DEF more of the other constituents.

At the bottom of the "S"s two horizontal lines are shown dotted. At one, marked "Ms" the hard Martensite *starts* to form, and below the line "Mf" this change is complete; the metal is all in the hard condition. For "silver steel" Ms lies at about 150°C However, Martensite cannot exist to the right of the line at "F".

Now, consider a piece of high-carbon steel at the point "Q". It is at about 780°C. If it cools slowly it will follow the line QP, taking perhaps 24 hours to cool down to 15°C. The line passes through both of the "S" curves, indicating that total transformation to Pearlite and Cementite has taken place. The material is

Principles of the Hardening Process 21

"annealed" – the steel has had time to go through all the changes we talked about earlier. Now look at the line QR. The metal has cooled through an identical temperature range, but this time in no more than one second. At no point does it cross the "S" curve, so that no transformation to Pearlite is possible. But it HAS crossed both the Ms and Mf lines, indicating that total transformation to Martensite has taken place. This sample is "hardened". These are examples of the two extremes, slow and fast cooling.

You will see on the diagram a line "QS", which JUST touches the nose of the left-hand "S" curve. This is the slowest rate – the "Critical" rate – of cooling which will achieve a fully hardened Martensitic condition. (The location of the point "S" will depend on

Fig. 16 A "Time-Temperature Transformation Diagram" ("S-Curve") for a high-carbon steel. Note – this is a typical curve only; the shape will vary from steel to steel.

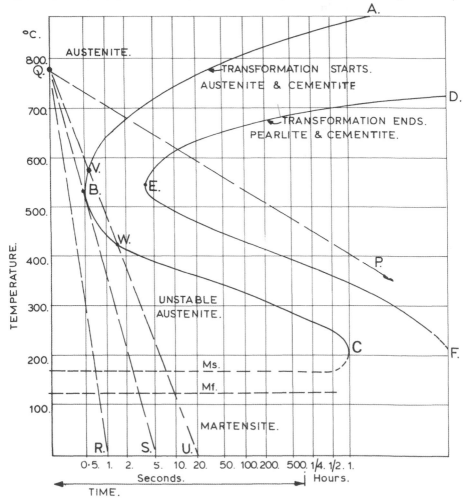

22 HARDENING, TEMPERING, AND HEAT TREATMENT FOR HOME MACHINISTS

the type of steel; it might typically be 2 or 3 seconds). The quench shown by the line "QU", however, *does* cross the "S" curve ABC, at "V" and "W", in and out again. Between "V" and "W" some of the Austenite will transform to Pearlite, but as the cooling curve only lies to the right of the line ABC momentarily the remainder will carry on down QU to form Martensite. The final state will, therefore, be mainly Martensite but with a little Pearlite as well. It will not be as hard, BUT, the presence of the Pearlite will make it less brittle and a bit tougher.**

This diagram helps us to understand what can happen in the center of a piece of steel during the quench. If it has a small cross-section, and is cooled along some line such as "QR", then the center of the section may follow a line between "QR" and "QS", and will be fully transformed right through; it will be "through hardened". If, however, it was a very thick piece the center might very well be cooled along "OU" even though the outside followed "QR". The center of the specimen would not be as hard as the outside – though it may well be tougher.

One of the purposes for which some of the alloying elements are added to modern "carbon" steels is the improvement of the "through hardening" characteristics; the alloy modifies the "S" curve. A plain, unalloyed carbon steel is not too good in this respect. But NO thick section of steel can be hardened right through, even when alloys *are* added. For "Silver Steel", which contains a little Chromium to help matters, the limit is 5/16 inch thick, though the loss of hardness at the center of a piece 3/8 inch thick is very small indeed. This "Limit to through Hardening" explains the difficulties sometimes met with when a large section carbon steel tool is ground down at the point to bring it to center-height in a small lathe, as in Fig. 17. The point of the tool is now located in the center of the section and will not be as hard as the original. The loss of hardness will be noticeable if a half-inch tool is ground down to 5/16 inch point-height. The cure is to anneal and reharden. See p.37.

DISTORTION DURING THE QUENCH

As well as hardness we are frequently concerned with the *shape* of the workpiece, especially when making gauges or form tools. A little thought will suggest that there is likely to be a dimensional change with all the transformations within the metal and that, in addition, the highly stressed crystals will "deflect" just as any stressed member will under load. Not only that – the very act of cooling causes a contraction and in a "quench" this contraction is sudden in the extreme. If the workpiece is not exactly symmetrical there is risk of uneven shrinkage.

**Note that it is not possible for any but an expert metallurgist to determine HOW MUCH Pearlite will be formed.

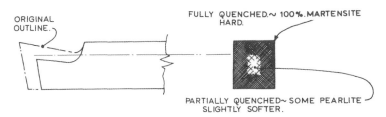

Fig. 17 *If a large-section carbon steel tool is ground down to suit a smaller lathe the new cutting edge will not be as hard as the original.*

The higher the cooling rate the greater the risk.

In cases where "shape" is important we must use a slower cooling rate, even though this may mean that the quench line for the center of the work may cross the nose of the "S" curve momentarily. Fortunately this is not so important in articles not intended for metal-cutting and in some cases can be an advantage, expecially for tools subject to shock loading. The risk of cracking is not great when dealing with (say) a simple "D"-bit, but can be acute in the case of a milling-cutter, with sharp corners at the tooth roots. In such a case it is prudent to sacrifice a little hardness in order to be sure of getting our tool in one piece, and a slower method of quenching must be sought.

In industry special methods are used, not necessarily beyond the capabilities of the model engineer, but they do need proper temperature control. The simplest method for us is to quench in *oil* instead of water. The risk of cracking and distortion is considerably reduced yet the loss of hardness is not great. If, however, distortion is of the first importance, as when making a gap gauge, then it is wiser to use the special oil-hardening tool-steel – "Ground Gauge Stock". (Though it can also be obtained in black bar as well). This material is alloyed so that oil-quenching always misses the knee of the "S" curve, and full transformation is obtained. It is not as hard as a water-hardened straight carbon steel, but is adequate for the purpose.

TEMPERING

Just as the "Good Shepherd" tempers the wind to the shorn lamb, so the prudent tool-maker tempers his hard steel against shock loads. A high-carbon tool steel,

properly heat treated, will have reached the maximum available hardness, but it will be very brittle. As I have tried to explain, the crystals are under considerable internal strain and any shock loading, or even rough handling, may cause fracture. This may apply occasionally even with oil-quenched steel. In addition, the grain size may not be as favorable to clean cutting action as we would like, especially if the initial temperature (point "Q" of Fig. 16) was not exactly right. If, however, we now reheat the steel to a relatively low temperature these crystals can be, to some extent, "stress-relieved" and if the temperature is held for a little while some degree of grain refinement may be had as well. For plain cutting tools, where shock loading is minimal, a very low tempering temperature will serve – the usual recommended is about 230°C, though this did refer to turning tools one or two inches square – I will have more to say about this later! It is, in addition, prudent to temper the tool-shank even more, so that it does not crack under the clamping forces of the tool-post.

Tempering can serve another purpose, though. We have seen that the quench produces Martensite – highly stressed Austenite crystals interspersed with needle-like Cementite. For some purposes, however, we need high strength and resilience rather than hardness as such – the classic case being the spring. There is no reason at all why a spring should be HARD; the engineer expects them to have a high yield stress and high resilience. Industrially it is possible to achieve this directly but this does need special equipment. (And, in any case, commercial springs are seldom made from straight carbon tool-steel). The only way open to most of us is to harden right out (preferably in oil) and then "temper back" to the desired condition. We reheat to, perhaps, 300°C – "blue". At this temperature the needles of Martensite change into little "nodules" and, of course, the crystals are completely stress relieved. The steel will be "hard" relative to mild steel, but nowhere near as hard as a cutting tool.

To sum up, we can modify the structure of our hardened steel to suit the purpose we have in mind by a secondary heat treatment at comparatively low temperatures. I will be covering the detail needs for various applications later, but you should bear in mind that "Tempering" serves three purposes: to stress relieve the "tight" crystals and so reduce the risk of cracking; to improve the grain size, so that you can get a sharp cutting edge; and, in some cases, to transform the Martensite to a nodular condition, to improve resilience. I will, in a later chapter, deal with this in more detail, especially in relation to the special needs of Ivory turner's tools, which must be brought up to a very fine polish and sharp edge.

ALLOY STEELS

Seventy-odd years ago, when the "Standard Practices" of model engineering were being established, carbon steel was just that – an alloy of carbon and iron. True, it would contain a few impurities, for the days of charcoal-smelted iron were over (though Holtzapffel was still using Huntsman crucible tool-steel made from imported Dannemorra charcoal iron) and typically 0.03% of sulfur and phosphorus was normal. Today, however, almost all steels contain other elements as well. We have already seen how drastically the characteristics of pure iron are altered by the addition of very small amounts of carbon and the same applies to these alloying

elements. The diagram (Fig. 13 on page 18.) is drawn for "plain" carbon steel, but each alloy will have a different characteristic equilibrium diagram, some very complex indeed.

Almost all carbon tool steels these days contain about 0.35% of Manganese, its main purpose being to counteract the effects of the impurity Sulfur. At this level the effect on fig. 13 and hence on the heat treatment is negligible. When present in higher amounts – 1% or more – the steel needs special treatment. A few tool-steels ("Silver" Steel is one – it contains no silver, by the way; the name refers to its appearance!) include about 0.5% of Chromium, partly to help in refining the grain size but also to improve "through hardening". At this level there is some slight effect on the shape of the diagrams, including the "S" curve, but no special treatment is needed. The-quenching temperature is slightly different, that is all. These steels are essentially "carbon" steels with *additives* to improve performance.

As the alloy content rises, however, and, more especially, when a combination of alloying elements is used, then the equivalent diagrams to Figs. 13 and 15 become very complicated indeed. (Chromium, for example, forms a very hard carbide on its own). When faced with a steel containing more than about 0.6% of any of these elements (and they can be Nickel, Chromium, Cobalt, Vanadium, Tungsten, Molybdenum, Titanium and others) the answer to the heat treatment problem is, for the model engineer, **"DON'T"**! A nice piece of 3% nickel 0.3% carbon steel will (if you are *sure* it is EN21) make excellent connecting rod bolts, but unless you have the exact heat treatment data it is best left in the "as supplied" state. Even more so if you come across any of the higher alloyed steels –

Principles of the Hardening Process   25

and even more so again if it has come from "Evans the Scrap". Heat treatment of such, without proper data and equipment, is likely to be disappointing if not catastrophic. (However, I will, in a later chapter, deal with the heat treatment of some of the medium carbon steels, which can, with care, be treated very effectively). Finally, don't forget that brazing, and to an even greater extent, welding, is a form of heat treatment!

SURFACE HARDENING

There are many situations, both in full-size and model engineering, where a hard-wearing surface is needed but the component also must resist shock loads – or perhaps repeated reversal of load, almost as bad. Cross-head and gudgeon pins are examples. The usual suggestion made by writers of articles in *Model Engineer* and elsewhere is to use Silver Steel, harden, and then temper back. This is not a very good solution to the problem. First, the tempering reduces the hardness of the wearing surface and, second, tempered Martensite is not the best material for a load-bearing component. Horses for courses! A Bugatti type 37 does not make the best of town carriages, and you would be hard put to it to make an "O" gauge loco on an

18-inch tool-room lathe, no matter how accurate it was.

The answer is to use a mild or medium carbon steel, of specification appropriate to the loading conditions, and then to modify the surface layer of the metal so that it can be hardened. You will remember that the earliest method of manufacture of high carbon steel involved its heating in the presence of carbon. This took a long time, but if we carry out the same process for a *short* time then the carbon will penetrate only a short distance. For models we only need a thin layer – perhaps as small as 0.005in. would serve – and this is what is achieved by "CASE-HARDENING". There are various ways in which it can be done, some which don't involved anything more than a blowlamp and some special compound, but all are practical for the model engineer. Once this surface layer has been carburised the part can be heated and quenched and, in most cases, does not need any tempering. The result is a core which is strong and tough, and a surface which is almost glass-hard. Further, the process is very flexible, and it is possible to harden selectively, and even to carry out machining operations on one part of a component after another part has been surface hardened. I give more details of the procedure on page 64.

26 HARDENING, TEMPERING, AND HEAT TREATMENT FOR HOME MACHINISTS

CHAPTER 3

Heating and Quenching in Practice

In this chapter I will deal with the practical aspects of Heat Treatment, but I am leaving detail discussion of the actual heating devices till later. For the purpose of this chapter, therefore, I will assume that your source of heat is, like the engine of your Rolls-Royce, "adequate for its purpose". I am going to leave the consideration of *Tempering* to the next chapter, too, as this is really a separate issue.

The Material. The first – and imperative – necessity is to decide what material you are hardening. If you are not sure about this – if it is just a "piece of good stuff" you have picked up from Evans the Scrap – then my advice is "Don't". I have by me as I write this the SAE list of steels which MIGHT be found in a scrap motor-car these days. If typed out on paper 7 inches wide the list would be several feet long. Less than one fifth are "plain" carbon steels – all the rest are more or less highly alloyed – and even if you knew that your piece was carbon steel it had probably been heat treated already and would require proper annealing before rehardening. The chances of finding any steel safe to heat treat on a scrap-heap these days are slim. Far better to start with a new piece of stock; after all, if you

are going to heat treat it it must be for some fairly important purpose.

However, there are cases where metal of more or less known provenance can be recycled, and if you are in a tight spot and cannot get new steel, then the following table may help in suggesting the probable carbon content of old tools etc. I emphasize the word "old", for these days even the humble cold chisel may be made from a non-tempering nickel alloy.

% Carbon	Type of Tools
0.7	Crowbars; Pickaxes; Screwdrivers
0.8	Large Masonry chisels; Quarry rock-drills; Wood-splitting Wedges
0.9	Cold Chisels; Shear-blades; Blacksmith's hot setts;
1.0	Smaller Cold Chisels; Old woodworking machine cutters; Handsaws.
1.1-1.2	Engineer's cutting tools; Drills; Reamers etc.
1.2-1.3	Files;
1.3-1.4	Razors; Engraver's tools; Saw-files.
1.4 up	Wire-drawing dies; Cold Saws.

Many of these could be made from high-speed steel, but this can easily be distinguished by using the "Spark Test" – see the *Model Engineer's Handbook.* In any case, however, the material should first be annealed (See page 71.) and a small test piece then sawn off and test-hardened with the estimated carbon content as a guide.

Heating We have already seen the need for slow heating, and I cannot emphasize this need sufficiently. The question is "How slow?" If put into a cold muffle furnace and heated up with the muffle, this will suffice. With the average muffle, in fact, the work will heat up slowly enough if put into the furnace when it is already at the hardening temperature. (In some books you will find this called the "Austenising Temperature", by the way). If you are using a molten lead or salt bath then it is necessary to preheat the work a little anyway, as I explain later. But with the ordinary blow-lamp or gas torch some care IS needed. It is all too easy to overheat thin parts locally. I find I take about five or six minutes to bring a small tool – about ⅜ inch × 3 inch long – up to the arrest point, and it takes a little longer to climb the remaining 60°C or so. This gives good results, and can be taken as a guide. Better to be too slow than too fast. At the arrest point there is a temptation to turn up the gas, as the metal seems to be making no progress. This is just the wrong thing to do! The little atoms are in process of moving house, and won't welcome being hurried over the job! Keep heating at a steady rate and when the metal starts to color up further you are very nearly at the right temperature. Overall, the short answer is that you must use your judgment, and try to get as much experience as you can, if you rely on torch or kitchen fire heating. For the odd D-bit that will be used once and then scrapped the heating rate may not be all that critical, but you MUST pay attention if the tool is an important one, likely to be used for years.

Once up to temperature you must hold the heat for some time. Again – "How long"? You have both to make sure that the metal is hot right to the center, AND give those atoms time to drift to their new spot. Fortunately in this case the answer is definite; metallurgists and generations of blacksmiths over a century or more have established the rule: heat for **ONE HOUR PER INCH OF THICKNESS,** once the tool is up to the hardening temperature. This means that a ⅜inch thick tool should be heated for about 20 minutes. Yes, I know! You have *never* held the heat for as long as this! I am sorry, but that means that you have never achieved the maximum possible hardness, either! Just to persuade you I have set up specially and hardened four pieces of carbon steel from the same bar, holding the temperature for one, five, ten, and fifteen minutes, the last being "right" for the ¼-inch stock used. The hardness, measured on my "vintage" Shore Scleroscope came out at 74, 76, 78, and 81, respectively. Those who know their hardness numbers will realize that these figures are all low – but equally, they will realize that the "Shore" is not suitable for such small specimens. A subsequent test on the last speciment showed a hardness of above 900 Vickers, and this is about right. The reduction in hardness for the shorter heating times is very evident – the "one minute piece" is softer "as hardened" than the tool should be when tempered.

It is true that our tools are relatively small compared with those formerly used in industry – or today, for that matter. They don't contain much metal – but their surface area is small, too, and the RATE of heat transmission needed to get even a ¼-inch tool to full temperature at the center in 15 minutes is very high. Clearly for the odd scriber-point it isn't all that important, but for cutting tools it does matter. I will, later, be telling

28 HARDENING, TEMPERING, AND HEAT TREATMENT FOR HOME MACHINISTS

you about the use of a molten salt-bath for heating, and one of the great advantages of this type of furnace is that the soaking time can be reduced; the rate of heat transfer is much better. Setting the work in a cold muffle furnace and letting it heat up with the furnace is good practice, too, for the muffle heating rate is about the same as that for the metal. You can halve the heating time in this way.

The Right Temperature. At first sight it might be assumed that we need to take the metal up to above the upper critical temperature – the line ABC of Fig 13, – but this is not the case. First (for high carbon tool-steels, that is) we do need some "Free Cementite" when we quench, and this does not appear until the metal has fallen below the upper critical temperature. Second, experience shows that the grain size is more favorable if the metal is quenched from a lower temperature. As a general rule steels having 1% carbon content or more are quenched from below the upper critical and those below 0.9% from above it. This is a "general" rule – there may be special reasons for departing from it – and one consequence is that the quench temperature does not vary much over the whole range of carbon content. Note that for heat treating OTHER than for pure hardening this may not apply – see Ch.VII.

The following table is drawn up from a number of "authorities" for steels all of which contained about 0.35% manganese – what today is regarded as a "straight" carbon steel. The exception is the "Silver Steel", which contains also about 0.45% Chromium.

Carbon, %	Temperature, °C
0.7 –0.85	790–800
0.86–1.05	770–780
1.06–1.25	770–780
Above 1.25	760–770
"Silver Steel"	770–790

These temperatures are for quenching in water or brine. For oil-quenching the metal is best heated perhaps 10-20°C higher, but I do not advise going above 800°C, FILE STEEL, usually 1.25% carbon with 0.5% chromium, gives maximum hardness from 800°, but it must not be heated much above this figure.

In all cases it is much better to obtain the correct quenching temperature from the manufacturers or the retailers if the best results are to be obtained. You will not go far wrong with the figures given in the table, but as is always the case "Perfection demands more care". If the EN No., or the newer numbers from BS 970/1972 (which, incidentally, incorporate the carbon content in the specification number) is known, then reference to the British Steel Corporation may produce the required information. (Look in the telephone directory, or try BSC, Swinden House, Rotherham S60 3AR). If the SAE number (Society of Automotive Engineers of America) is known, then data is given in their handbook, which should be available in the local reference library. This gives almost ALL steels made to U.S. specifications, and they don't differ much from BS 970; many have the same number. In the case of the oil-hardening gauge steels the proper temperatures are given on the wrapper.

As a final point of comfort, these temperatures are not critical to a few degrees; most steelmakers give a range, if only because there is a tolerance on the actual carbon content. If you are within 10°C you will not be far wrong, PROVIDED you hold the steel there for the proper length of time.

Judging the Temperature. This is what separates the men from the boys! The old-timers could

Heating and Quenching in Practice 29

estimate almost to a degree just by looking at the steel, but they were hardening carbon steel all day long. If you have a gas or electric furnace which is equipped with a pyrometer you are in no difficulty – provided that you check the accuracy of the instrument now and again. (If it has no pyrometer I give some hints on making one on page 107.) With gas or fire heating we have to rely on the color of the metal. Now, make no mistake; this is an EXACT measure of the temperature – in fact, one form of pyrometer makes use of the color. The frequency of vibration of the atomic structure is a direct function of the absolute temperature, and this frequency determines the color of the light which is emitted. The problem lies in how to *describe* the color. The birds in my garden probably would not recognize your cherries as being red at all! And, for that matter, some readers may have blue blood in their veins! Only experience can give you a proper judgment. For what it is worth, generations of blacksmiths over a thousand years or so have adopted the following "names" for the colors as seen in a relatively dim light. (But NOT, on any account, under light from a fluorescent tube, which makes a pig's ear of any color judgment).

700°C	Dull Red
750°C	Blood Red
800°C	Cherry Red
825°C	Bright Cherry Red
850°C	Red
900°C	Bright Red
1000°C	Yellow-red

The best thing to do is to find someone who has a muffle furnace with pyrometer, or arrange a club visit to the local Technical College, and have the furnace brought up to the various temperatures so that you can see what it really looks like.

(Have a piece of clean steel set in place – don't rely on the appearance of the furnace chamber). There is no substitute for this type of experience. However, to help you I have taken some color photographs of a chunk of steel in my own muffle, and the printer has done his excellent best to reproduce these on page 33. As a further guide, I find that the larger boiling ring (one of the spiral type) on our Creda 90R electric cooker reached and stabilized at 780°C after running full on for 15 mins. with no pan over it; and the firebed of a Courtier Type 8R closed stove, burning "Phurnacite" (the egg-shaped things) lay between 1000 and 1100°C after about 15 minutes drawing up the fire, the firebed being about 7 inches deep.

There are a few other guides. The lower critical temperature is an "arrest point" at which the color will seem to hang back. This is an indication that you are within about 50°C of the required temperature. (In passing, provided you are *above* this arrest point you will get some hardening effect, but none if you are below it). Very near to this arrest point – very slightly below – lies the "Curie Point" (about 770°C) at which the steel ceases to be magnetic. You can keep checking with a magnet or, as I do, use a small compass. Be careful, though; neither magnets nor compasses like heat, and there is a risk that the magnet may pick up a small workpiece and refuse to let go!

There are some "Temperature Indicating Crayons" available, of two types. One changes color when the temperature marked on the packet is reached; the other is "stroked" over the work and if it melts within two seconds the temperature is as indicated; if longer it is too low, and if shorter, too high. Both are pretty accurate provided they haven't been in stock for years, but they do need a little practice in

30 HARDENING, TEMPERING, AND HEAT TREATMENT FOR HOME MACHINISTS

use. Mine are made by the "Markal Company" – an American firm. Another well-known brand is Tempilstik and is available in a range of temperatures from 40 to 1200°C. It is widely available both online an in welding equipment stores. For use in muffle furnaces without pyrometers the well-known "Seeger Cones" (Wengers Ltd, Etruria, Stoke on Trent) can be used. These curl over at the top when the right temperature is reached, and are used in pottery kilns, where careful temperature control is equally important. They have the disadvantage that they can be used only the once, so that you need them by the dozen.

A sense of proportion must be maintained in all this, as in all aspects of heat treatment. If you make the odd form tool or punch once or twice a year, then the photos on pp. 33–35 showing the heating colors will meet all your needs. And, for unimportant jobs, provided the temperature lies between the two critical points (i.e. for Silver Steel, between 730°C and 830°C) you will get SOME hardening effect, though not very good at the extremes. If you harden tools fairly frequently then you will very soon develop the color sense which will enable you to work by eye; in any case, you have to judge the color under *your* workshop conditions, not those of an industrial heat treatment shop. But, if you make all your own tools and gauges, and are hardening machinery parts as well, then you would be well advised to look out for a secondhand muffle-furnace (or even a new one!) or look at some of the other arrangements I detail in a later chapter.

Scaling. This is of little importance in a lathe tool, as it must be ground in any case, but if it is a form-tool, which has a profile which cannot be formed on the grinding wheel, it can be a nuisance, if not a difficulty. If using a muffle the scaling can be reduced by setting a few pieces of *dry* charcoal at the mouth of the muffle, just against the door. This will consume any oxygen in the muffle – or most of it – and reduce that available to oxidise the metal. (Don't use coke or coal). Alternatively there are some "Antiscale Paints" available. These are used by ceramic enamellers, but are equally effective in protecting steel. It is painted on the work and is effective up to around 800°C. I use it very successfully, but also use a substitute. This is ordinary whitening (powdered chalk) mixed with water or methylated spirit and painted on. Sometimes I bind iron wire over the top, and clart that up with the paste as well. (The wire must, of course, be pulled off before quenching) This is effective also. Both have the disadvantage that the paint or chalk tends to "incandesce" and so prevents proper color judgment. No matter in a muffle, but fatal if using a torch. The answer to this is to have an identical piece of scrap steel (it need not be carbon steel) alongside and provided you ensure that both the workpiece and the test specimen are equally heated the latter can be used to judge the color. Horologists coat their small parts with soft soap when heating. This is said to avoid scaling too, but I must confess I have not used it myself.

QUENCHING

There are three quenching mediums in common use; plain water, brine, and oil. Water is cheap and easy to obtain, and will serve almost all the model engineer's needs. Brine gives a somewhat better hardening effect and can give more even cooling – the results are more uniform. Oil is essential when quenching complex shapes – the slight loss of hardness is accepted as a fair exchange for the reduced risk of distortion and cracking.

The actual cooling process with the three quenchants is different – it is not just a case of difference in *degree* of quench. With plain water the initial effect is the generation of steam all over the workpiece. This causes an intense and sudden cooling effect, as the latent heat of vaporisation of water is very high. However, this results in the workpiece being blanketed in a steam jacket and steam is a very poor conductor of heat. The cooling rate would drop dramatically if this insulating coating were not removed. So, the work must be *agitated* in the bath; if this is done, then cooling proceeds at a fairly rapid and steady rate until the approach to 100°C. (As we will see later, once the temperature has fallen to about 300°C the rate of cooling is not important).

In the case of Brine a similar procedure takes place, but the presence of the salt in the water seems to retard the formation of the steam blanket. For some reason the cooling appears to be more even but it is faster – about twice as fast as water down to 300°C or thereabouts. Brine is invariably used for "water" quenching steels in industry, and the figures quoted for hardness in commercial specifications all assume that the work was quenched in 10% salt/water brine.

Oil behaves very differently. (Assuming a proper "Cold Quenching Oil" is used. "Motor Oil" will have very unpredictable results). It is slower in the initial cooling, because oil has a much lower latent heat than water. Once the "vapor blanket" starts to form, however, the cooling rate (with the same degree of agitation) is very little different from that of water. Below 400°C, however, the oil cools the work very much slower. Using a test rig, it was found (with still, unagitated fluids) that water would take about 3½ seconds to reduce the temperature of a standard probe from 800°C to 420°C, and oil about 5 seconds – no great difference. But whereas the water-cooled probe only needed a total of 5 seconds to fall to 200°C, oil took 25 seconds. This means that both fluids bring the steel through the lower critical temperature at about the same rate – oil slight slower; both are rapid enough to prevent the transformation to Pearlite. However, the much slower rate of cooling in the lower reaches – below 400°C – with oil means that the transformation to Martensite takes place in a much more leisurely fashion, and this reduces the risk of distortion and cracking considerably. The Martensite will form anyway, even if we air cooled from (say) 200°C. This test was, of course, under artificial conditions; the metal would not be properly hardened even with the water – we need cooling rates of thousands of degrees/minute through the critical range for that – but it does give an indication of the different behavior of the two fluids. Agitation will reduce the time taken, but the character of the cooling curve will be similar.

For model engineers, therefore, we can say that in general water will serve for our needs, but brine is preferable when ultimate hardness is needed. Oil should be used for milling cutters and for gauges or hardened jigs – preferably using the proper oil-hardening steel for the latter, as it is formulated to avoid distortion. The brine is made from "Vacuum-dried Salt" – the coarse kind used by farmers for butter; cheaper than domestic salt, and without the additives, some of which may not be desirable for a quench-bath. An 8 to 10% solution is general – 12-16oz/gallon or 80-100gm/liter. In use, some of the water will evaporate and this must be made up. An old test was that a fresh potato would

32   HARDENING, TEMPERING, AND HEAT TREATMENT FOR HOME MACHINISTS

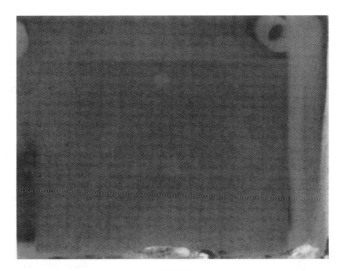

700°C

725°C

Indications of color/temperature using a 3 × 4 in. steel plate photographed in the author's muffle furnace.

Heating and Quenching in Practice 33

750°C

780°C

A difficulty with printing a color reference is that the result is reflected light; the original color is radiated light.

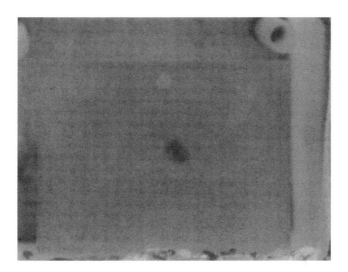

800°C

840°C

For greatest accuracy, these color samples should be viewed 2 ft. away from a 60W pearl bulb indirectly reflected by a silver shade.

> **Publisher's Note:** See inside back cover for color chart and inside front cover for photo example.

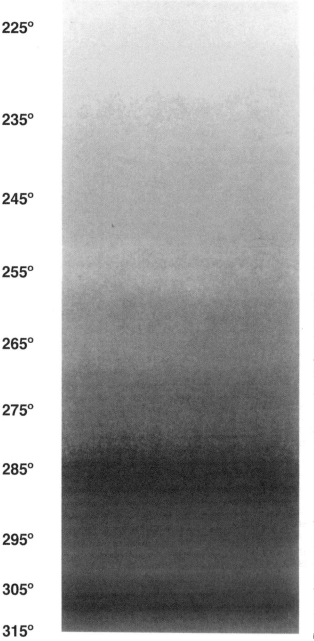

225°

235°

245°

255°

265°

275°

285°

295°

305°

315°

These tempering temperature colors are very accurate and were produced by Steve Archibald (Argus artist) from tempered sample discs carefully prepared by the author.

36 HARDENING, TEMPERING, AND HEAT TREATMENT FOR HOME MACHINISTS

just float in it, but you can easily make up a simple test hydrometer if you want to be fussy.

A plastic tube is weighted so that it floats with the top about ¾ inch above the surface in plain water. It is then calibrated by setting it in brine of differing strengths. If you start with the quench bath at 8%, and let it down when it tops 10% you will be within the not very important limits.

Decarburisation. Occasionally one finds a tool that has been properly treated, everything as it should be, but somehow it does not seem to be hard. A file can "touch" it. However, any attempt to saw it in two results in a sawblade with no teeth on it! The cause is surface decarburisation – the outer skin of the metal has lost some of its carbon content, and it is not hardenable steel any more. This is the origin of the old blacksmith's rule "forge large and grind small". The tool was always forged oversize, so that any decarburised surface would have to be ground off. The problem is not acute for the model engineer, as he is not heating tools with shanks up to a couple of inches square, but it can happen.

It is caused by the action of oxygen on the metal, and this is one reason for avoiding the use of oxy-gas heating flames. It can also be caused by scale; you will recall from Ch.I. that Wrought Iron was made by the reaction of iron oxide with the carbon in the cast iron. The remedy is, of course, to avoid scaling in the first place, as suggested above. I have very little trouble with tools around ⁵⁄₁₆ to ⅜ inch square, but the few half-inch ones were all made deliberately about ¹⁄₃₂ inch oversize at the point to permit sufficient grinding down.

Overheating. This can arise from several causes. The first – sheer forgetfulness, when the work is left in the muffle too long – we can ignore; the cure is up to you!

Local overheating is almost inevitable if oxy-acetylene is used, and I go into this in more detail later. This type can be irreparable, with oxide inclusions forming in the grain boundaries, rendering the steel useless for anything but as a missile. The commonest difficulty, though, is with workpieces which are either very thin or which have a very uneven cross section. The scriber-point is just such a case; it is impossible to heat the tapered section evenly. The remedy here is to form the taper and the point by grinding *after* heat treatment. For other cases – e.g., where there is a small protrusion on a larger mass – the remedy is to fit a "heat sink". A piece of scrap steel with a hole in it (not too large a piece; something in proportion to the main mass of metal) is set over the delicate part, and the whole heated up as one. The slender part is protected from the direct heat of the flame, and will reach the proper temperature just the same, both by conduction from the main body and by radiation from the shield. The protecting shield must, of course be removed before quenching. No problem arises, of course, with furnace heating.

Metal which is overheated will almost certainly crack on the quench. The best procedure is to stop work, anneal the piece, and start again. If, however, the steel has been brought up badly over temperature – yellowy-red, for example – then it will need reforging before it will be any use again. If it has gotten hotter than this, throw it away; it won't be any use – not as tool steel, anyway.

Whether water, brine, or oil is used, some debris will collect in the bottom of the tank. In the case of oil this may include some sludge, which might interfere with the quench. In industry elaborate methods are used to keep the baths clean, but for us, simpler methods are suitable. For water, just pour it away

Heating and Quenching in Practice 37

and use fresh. Brine may be kept longer (in plastic containers, not metal) and then flushed down the sink with plenty of water. It should last a long time anyway. Oil is more precious and costly, but a simple strainer can be used to remove the dirt. Keep a lid on the oil-bath when not in use. I find that even after two years my own oil-bath seldom needs cleaning, and I use oil more than most model engineers.

The proper oil should be used if at all possible. There are various grades, and each oil company has its own. I use B.P. "Quendila A22", though the "Quendila 19" is almost as good and cheaper. It is unfortunate that these oils are no longer supplied in the old one gallon cans, but a 25 liter (about 5 gallon) drum can be shared between friends – and a 400 liter drum could be cheaper still for club purchase. Failing a special oil, a good "Spindle Oil" of about SAE10 to 20 viscosity will serve. But NOT motor oil, which is blended for different service and characteristics, and *most emphatically* NOT "used" motor oil. This is downright dangerous; it can contain up to 25% of the heavier fractions of gas and can flash off into a furious fire if used for quenching hot metal.

The size of the quench bath must accord with the size (and quantity) of the work passing through at any one time. Whether water, brine, or oil, the amount should be 1 gallon per lb of hot metal (10 liters/kg) to avoid undue temperature rise. A half-inch tool 5 inches long weighs about 0.35lb. For the odd center punch and similar small casual jobs I keep a large "Golden Syrup" can, as these have good lids, but for serious work a plastic "builder's bucket" does very well. (They can be had with lids). This will hold up to two gallons and is very robust – it will even withstand the *occasional* accident with hot metal on the plastic! I have a larger can for oil, which once held emulsion paint; this has a lid, but I am sorry to find that present day paint cans have very bad tops. Mine holds about ¾ gallon, which is very adequate for all the work I do.

The initial temperature of the bath should not be too cold. True, you get a better quench the colder it is (I have an account of tools quenched in freezing cold mercury!) but you do have to compromise against the risk of cracks. Something between 20°C and 30°C is about right. However, in the summer I just use tap water which has stood in the workshop for a while; in winter I draw some from the hot tap. Oil should be at about 25°C. These figures are not critical – no need to go around with precision thermometers to measure them! A useful point to note is that brine or water at 70°C will give a similar effect to that obtained from cold oil and if you have problems with a workpiece constantly cracking in the hardening and have no oil you could try heating the water/brine to 50°C. A quench in water at 90°C will not harden at all, but it can toughen the steel a little. The cooling in this case is almost certain to cross the "S" curve, with some Pearlite formation.

Quenching Technique. This does require some attention. Far too many people set the work in the water and swirl it about violently. The recommendation seen in some books that the water in the bucket be set in rotary motion and the tool taken down vertically at one side is even more unfortunate. Look at Fig.18. The water is passing the work (or the work is passing through the water – same effect) with the result that there is a reduction in water pressure on the downstream side. This means that steam will form more readily on that side and it will be underquenched. There is plenty of motion to displace steam at the front, and perhaps

38 HARDENING, TEMPERING, AND HEAT TREATMENT FOR HOME MACHINISTS

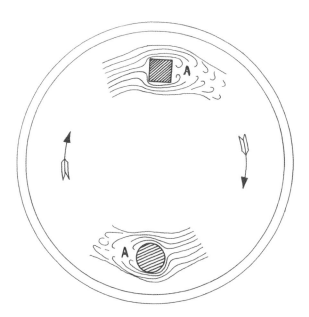

Fig. 18 *Quenching. If the flow of water past the work is fast enough to cause eddies at AA steam formation on the downstream side will be aggravated.*

at the sides, but very little at the back. Distortion is inevitable; indeed, skilled filehardeners use this phenomenon to straighten a file which has bent in the heating! The preferred method is a relatively SLOW circular motion of the work, combined with an equally fairly slow vertical up and down motion, so that the work travels on a helical path through the quenchant. All sides get equal treatment. The motion should be just enough to remove steam bubbles as they form – no more. Anything more violent than that does more harm than good.

For a long and slender object – say a broach – even this gentle rotary motion may be too much. In which case you must be content with a simple up-and-down movement; again, fast enough to remove steam bubbles but no more. You must try this for yourself – a little experiment is better than several pages of mine. The object is to remove the steam bubbles in the middle part of the quench – or the vapor blanket in the case of oil. With a very large object you may have to move it more, but still gently, to avoid hot coolant, but clearly a large piece needs a larger quench tank, and you should not try to get away with an inadequate volume of coolant. In industry, of course, elaborate systems of propellers, underwater jets, and so on, are used to get a controlled but random movement of the coolant, in which the work can simply be lowered. Even so, it does need a lot of experiment, and it is interesting to know that the best files – even though made by the thousand – are still hand quenched in brine.

There is just one point about the oil quench which may be helpful. I find that a deepish bath is better than one of the same volume but "fatter". This means that the type of workpiece which needs an oil quench can be moved more in a vertical direction than otherwise. In many cases I find that no rotary motion is needed at all.

Stage Quenching The critical part of the quench is to get the work reduced in temperature past the knee of the "S" curve (Fig 15, just to remind you!) Once past this point the cooling can be quite a bit slower – Martensite will still form. This being so there would seem to be no reason why we should not remove the work from the bath once it has gotten down to, say, 300 to 350°C, and cool the rest of the way in a second bath. This is done in commercial plants almost universally. It has several advantages. The primary bath does not heat up so much – important if you have a number of pieces to quench. If using brine, the second bath can be clean water, which will remove most of the salt, and there will be less evaporation from the brine bath itself. There is no need for agitation in this second bath – the metal can take its own time. The only care you must take is to avoid dropping the workpiece, especially if it is fragile. It will be pretty brittle at this stage.

Partial Quenching There is no need to quench the whole of a large workpiece (nor need to heat the whole of it for that matter) if only part needs hardening. After reforging the end of my pickaxe, for example – an act which will have annealed it, as the forging temperature is about 950°C – I first heat up to between "Blood" and "Cherry" red and quench just the end 6 inches, the point is then briskly rubbed with a broken grindstone, with the hot part laid on my small anvil to act as a heat-sink. Then, when the point is clean, I hold it to the light until the colors run up to temper the point. Thus the point is hard and tempered, but the main body of the head is relatively soft. I will be expanding on Tempering in the next chapter, but can say now that this procedure is very legitimate, though nowadays one would be happier (for important tools) if the temper heat could be held for longer.

To sum up. We must heat the metal slowly, both to ensure that it is hot right through and so that the transformations needed have sufficient time to take place. We must "soak" the metal at the hardening temperature, choosing the temperature appropriate to the material being used. The "quench" should follow immediately, and this must be done in a manner which removes steam bubbles without causing violent eddies in the cooling medium. And the quench tank must be proportioned to the size and quantity of the work in hand. If all this is in order you should get optimum hardness every time! It only remains to temper it, and this we deal with in the next chapter.

CHAPTER 4

Tempering

The need for tempering has been discussed in Ch.II, and to some extent the degree of temper also. But while the quench temperature is fairly easily determined, depending mainly on the carbon content of the steel, the tempering temperature depends almost entirely on the use to which the tool will be put. It is not even sufficient to say "Lathe Tools" for the temper needed (say) for turning EN1A will be very different from that appropriate to a tool to cut chilled cast iron. The effect, as we have already seen, is to improve the "toughness" – resistance to shock – at the expense of some of the hardness. A tool not subject to shock, such as a file, may not be tempered at all, while a spring will be tempered almost to soft. It follows that considerable personal judgment must be used, if only to take account of the work normally done in the shop. One reason for using carbon steel tools instead of HSS (apart from the fact that they *are* harder) is that it is very easy to temper to suit the work.

The change in toughness and hardness has already been mentioned, but I show a further diagram in Fig 19. I must emphasize that the actual *shape* of the curves will vary from steel to steel, with some, for example, showing a "peak"

of toughness at a relatively low temper. It must be said, too, that the loss of hardness may be more apparent than real, and is difficult to put a number to. Indeed, the point of a lathe tool may well show a variation of two points on the Rockwell scale over the surface. (Hardness testing numbers and their determination are considered in Ch.8.)

There is a further point, and one which I believe is often overlooked. Just as quoted cutting speeds in Production Engineering textbooks are geared to industrial, not model engineering, conditions, so are the recommended tempering temperatures in toolmaker's catalogs and metallurgy textbooks. The temper they suggest for a carbon steel lathe tool, for example, assumes that it will be in use for a full series of shifts over a 44 hour week. (Actually, probably a 56 hour week at the time the book was written!) Some of my form tools have had no more than half-an-hour's work in twenty years! So – use your judgment, bear in mind the discussion in Ch.II, and, above all, *experiment*. The premier model engineering club, is after all, the "Society of Model and *Experimental* Engineers"!

Temperatures. Having said all that, I will try to give some help in the form of guidelines in the table below. I have run

Tempering   41

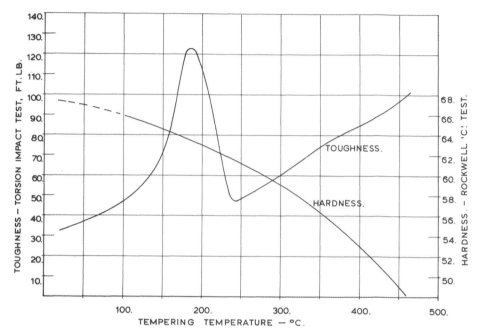

Fig. 19 *Effect of tempering on the mechanical properties of a brine-quenched 1.15% carbon steeel.*

into quite a difficulty over this, as different authorities, different steelmakers, and different users quote varying tempers for the same tools. In particular, American reference books seem to give figures 10 to 15°C higher than do European ones. This may be due to the different steel specification, but I suspect it is probably because, at the end of the 19th century, when much of the work was

TEMPERING TEMPERATURES FOR VARIOUS TOOLS

Arbors	200°C	Dies (Drawing)	200°C	Pickaxe	255-275°C
Axe, Cutting edge	255	Drill (Very small)	210	Planer Tools	215-225
Brass-turning tools	170-190	Drill (Small)	220-240	Reamers	230-240
Chasers (Thread)	230	Drill (Large)	245	Scrapers	200
Chilled iron-turning	150	Engraver's tools	230-250	Taps	210-220
Cold Chisel	260-280	Gauges	220	Screwdrivers	280-290
Counterbore	220-240	Hammer-head	230-250	Shaper Tools	215-225
Centers (Lathe)	215	Lathe Tools**	200-220	Springs	300-310
Dies (Screwing)	215-225	Milling Cutters	210-230	Wood Chisels	215-225

NOTES (1) ** See comment in the text on lathe tools
       (2) "Silver Steel" may be tempered at slightly lower figures than plain carbon steel.

first published, American firms worked their machines harder than we did. In the table I have tried to iron out these differences, but where in doubt I have tended toward the lower figures, to take account of the lighter duty cycle of model engineers' tools.

These temperatures are, traditionally, associated with "Tempering colors", and many publications simply refer to "straw" or "blue" instead of quoting the actual figure in °C. The following can be used as a guide, but again, there are slight differences between different publications. There is also a problem in interpretation; what kind of straw, for example!

tempers we have been advised to use in the past are far too high. When the accepted practice was first established carbon steel tools were universally used, both by model engineers and in industry. Tool sections were large – a 3½ inch Britannia was *designed* for half-inch tools – and we used industrial practice where, as I have already pointed out, the cutting edges were subject to an 8 or 10 hour day.

It is obvious that we must temper down the shank, otherwise the clamping forces will cause fracture, but the actual cutting edge is seldom subject to any shock load – on a lathe tool, at least; the case of planer or shaper tools is different. Now,

Yellow	215°C	Light Purple	275°C	
Pale Straw	225°C	Dark Purple	285°C	
Straw	235°C	Dark Blue	295°C	*A color chart*
Dark Straw	245°C	Blue	305°C	*for tempering colors appears on page 36.*
Reddish dark straw	255°C	Pale Blue	315°C	
Brown-red	265°C	Gray	Above about 330°C	

These colors are as viewed in daylight or strong tungsten lamp electric light. They will be at fault if judged under a fluorescent tube. We will look at the use of color-tempering in more detail later in the chapter.

Special case of lathe tools. First, let us think again about what we are doing. The object of tempering is to increase the toughness – resistance to shock and chipping – even though this means a slight loss of hardness. Clearly, in a center punch the risk of damage from blows is considerable. But in the case of lathe tools, WHEN EMPLOYED ON THE KIND OF WORK DONE BY MODEL ENGINEERS, I would suggest that the

the cutting edge is subject to heating. We can use a higher cutting speed with "High Speed Steel" simply because its tempering temperature lies between 600 and 700°C; some grades will still cut when red-hot. We use lower speeds with carbon steel because if the tool point does get at all hot it will "Temper down" and soften. Clearly, the lower the initial tempering temperature the less risk of damage to the tool point from wear. And the harder the tool point is to begin with, the longer it will take to heat it up to danger point when (in effect) it "tempers itself" and loses hardness.

For these reasons my practice for some time has been to temper lathe tools very

Tempering 43

lightly – just sufficient to effect a little grain refinement and to give some stress relief to the crystal structure; there is still some marked increase in toughness. I first temper the *whole tool* at between 180°C and 200°C, and then "let down" the shank *only* at around 280°C while keeping the tool point cool either in a bath of water or by using the ancient device of sticking the business end into a new-dug potato. This gives excellent results, both with "Silver Steel" and with a straight 1.15% carbon steel. I use an even more refined method for my Ivory-turning tools and those for slide-rest work when "ornamentally turning" in exotic wood, and this is dealt with on page 74.

Tempering Procedure. To be properly effective the tempering process must be given time to work and we are also faced, as in the case of heating before quenching, with the need to be sure that the tool is hot right through. If we have a tempered surface with a brittle core we have not really reduced the risk of cracking under load at all. The rule is the same – ONE HOUR PER INCH OF THICKNESS, though this is not as important in the case of a tool shank, where any temper between 260 and 290°C will serve. For the tool point, of course, the rule applies to the thickness there, not that of the shank. Now, one of the virtues of the "classical" tempering method – allowing the heat to creep up the shank to the point – is that this heat travels, in the main, through the core of the tool; and provided the shank is heated gently enough, the "soaking time" will look after itself. Even so, there is a risk that the temper may not be complete; yes; I know it works, but it is so easy to make it "work better" and we should always try for perfection. We will look at this "easy method" in a moment.

Tempering should take place *as soon as is practicable* after quenching. The tool should, of course, have cooled to not more than 50°C, and cooling to room temperature is safer. The reason for this expeditious tempering is that the metal is under internal stress from the quench and if, as is most usual the workpiece has a "shape" as opposed to being just a block there is risk of spontaneous cracking arising from differential contraction as well. There is also a risk of "crazing" – time cracks; these can appear if a tool is left too long in the as-quenched condition.

This need for "haste" is one reason why horologists and gunsmiths like the "blazing off" procedure – the tempering takes place as soon as the work comes out from the quenching oil. If for any reason tempering must be delayed then it may help if the work is set in boiling water for a quarter of an hour or so before setting it aside to await the final treatment.

Heating for Tempering. First, the "easier way" mentioned above. Go and look at the cooker in the kitchen. You will see that it has a thermostat on the oven if gas or electric fired, or a built-in thermometer in it if fired by solid fuel. You will, I think, find that the thermostat goes up nearly to 300°C – certainly to 250°C – or to "Gas Mark 9". (Degrees Centigrade = 140 + 11 times the gas mark approximately) So, you have a good thermostatically controlled, or at least "temperature indicating", tempering furnace on the premises! The cookbook will give you the temperatures, and if you time things right you can set your tools in the oven alongside the joint. The table below gives the usual temperatures used in this kind of heat treatment shop, though the time may vary a bit depending on the judgment of the oven-shop forewoman.

44   HARDENING, TEMPERING, AND HEAT TREATMENT FOR HOME MACHINISTS

160°C	Irish stew 2h
180°C	Braised pigeon, 45m: Casseroles, 2½h: last stage of roast duck etc, 3h.
190°C	Roast chicken 20m/lb: last stage of roast beef, 15m/lb.
200°C	Cottage pie, 1½h: Mince pies, 25m Cheese straws, 15m.
220°C	Yorkshire pudding, 25m: most pies, 25m: First stage of roast duck or turkey, 20-30m.
230°C	Scones, 10m; Bread, 30-40m.
245°C	First stage of roast beef or pork, 20m.

In addition, you probably have a deep-frying chip-pan. Chips are cooked at 190°C for 5 minutes or so, and then "browned" at 195°C, but the oil can safely be taken up to about 200-210°C on an electric cooker. (One has to be careful on gas, as unless the oil is fresh there will spitting and some vapor).

If you compare the above with the table on page 42 you will see that this domestic workshop can temper many of your tools for you while performing its normal office, and it is only necessary to negotiate mutually acceptable terms with the proprietor! There is, of course, no reason (so far as I am concerned, anyway) why the oven or chip-pan should not be used "out of cooking hours" and in this connection it is worth noting that a tool which ought to be tempered at 200°C is often better treated if it is "cooked" for its full time at 190°C than if merely "heated till the colors run up". The frying oil, especially, is useful, as the heat transfer is excellent. The only caveat I would enter is that it would be prudent to use an oven or chip-pan thermometer, as the thermostat on domestic cookers can get out of calibration in time.

You can, of course, use "frying oil" as a tempering oil in the workshop, and you may still be able to obtain the special "Tempering Oils" which can be used to temperatures as high as is normally needed. (Quenching oil is not suitable). However, you do need a substantial container – a thin one may overheat the oil locally – and if using gas heating, a gentle flame, not the kind you would use for brazing.

The **Salt Bath** is the normal method of tempering used in industry. Tempering salts are very innocuous, being a mixture of Sodium Nitrite and Potassium Nitrate, (*Nitrite,* and *Nitrate*) which melts at 160°C. Again, you need a substantial container, and I use the outer vessel from an old-fashioned glue-pot. Fig 20 shows the setup; the old boiling ring I picked up at a sale for a few pence finally gave up, and you see the pot here on a replacement. Ordinary mercury thermometers, usually nitrogen filled, are available which go up to 400°C, and are not expensive – they can be had from laboratory equipment suppliers, or ordered through your local pharmacist. Alternatively the well-known "Rototherm" dial thermometers can be used. But for most of our work an oven thermometer from a scrapped cooker will go up high enough – though it may be marked in Fahrenheit.

The salts are marketed through Edgar Vaughan & Co., Legge Street, Birmingham and it may be that by the time this book is published the usual model engineer's suppliers will sell them in much smaller quantities. (Direct supply from Vaughans may involve a "Club purchase"). There are, of course, a number of brands, but the only kind I have used is the DEGUSSA type TS150/AS140. It comes as a powder of the consistency of domestic salt, but must be kept dry, as it can absorb moisture fairly quickly. It is non-toxic, and the only serious hazard is that, like some weedkillers, if absorbed into woodwork (or your overalls) it

Tempering 45

Fig. 20 *A simple tempering salt bath. The outer case of a cast-iron glue-pot is set on an electric boiling ring. Note the protective case on the thermometer. Normally a glass-fiber insulating blanket is wrapped around the pot, but was removed for the photograph.*

"supports combustion". I deal with "Safety" in heat treatment on page 102, and only mention this now to reassure you that we are not talking about material which is poisonous.

The great advantage of this method (like that using the oven) is that you have complete control of the temperature to within a degree or so. There is no problem with "time" – you can leave the work in as long as you like. And the actual time can be a bit shorter, as the heat transfer is very good indeed. The one thing you do have to watch is that there is no oil or water trapped in little holes, as this would be dangerous. The procedure is first to bring the bath up to the working temperature. The workpiece can be set alongside the pot to dry if you have any doubts about it being dry. (With oil-quenched work I usually wash in carbon tetrachloride or a similar degreasant). You need some means of holding the work – it is no fun groping about in hot molten salt to find it. A piece of wire wound around will serve. Immerse the metal slowly; you will notice that the temperature falls, but will slowly rise again – there is not, as a rule, any need to increase the heating rate. Leave the work in for the prescribed time, having an eye on the temperature; you may have to adjust the control switch from time to time, but if it stays within a few degrees this will be sufficient. The piece can be allowed to air-cool after the time is up – there is no need to "quench"; quenching is only necessary when, as in flame heating, stored heat in one part of the tool might overheat the part being tempered. Any salt which adheres can easily be washed off in warm water afterward.

Once you have tempered the tool overall in this way the shank can be "let down" with a gas torch, as I have previously explained. With milling cutters, D-bits, taps, dies, or any other complicated tools this is not necessary. In the case of long tools like reamers you may have to use a deep water-bath with some means of holding the tool upright in order to let down the driving square on the end.

The salt bath is the answer to almost all the problems met with in tempering. For complex shapes – especially milling cutters – it is almost the only way that the tool can be tempered properly, and size is no problem either, provided the pot is proportioned to the size of the work – you need about 10lb of salt for one lb of steel, but it isn't critical. You must, of course, remember that the tide will rise when the work goes in; don't fill the pot too full! Finally, a detail point on heating. When cold, a crust will form on the top of the salt. Initial heating must be slow, and it is advisable to apply just a little heat to the outside at the top of the pot to get a little melt around the crust. A lid should always be in place when restarting a salt pot.

Color Tempering. This is the method most model engineers are accustomed to. Obviously, even if you *have* a salt furnace it just isn't worth firing it up if all that needs treating is a rehardened screwdriver and there are many jobs in the average workshop for which sophisticated methods are not worth while. Of course, if you have no salt-bath, and the use of domestic oven and chip pan are denied you, then you must use "temper colors" to indicate the temperature. It cannot in any way be disdained as "bad practice"; the method has been used for centuries, for swords and pike-heads in the days before there were any lathe-tools.

The colors are formed by a film of oxide which is very thin indeed and which gets thicker as the temperature increases. It would seem that the color change is, in part, due to the light reflected from the surface of the metal itself passing through differing thicknesses of the oxide. Certainly the exact color does depend on both the type of metal and the surface finish. The difference between the color of "mild" steel and high-carbon steel is small, but is there, as is the difference between that of quenched and unquenched carbon steel. The effect is to give a variation in temperature for the same shade, but this is only the odd degree centigrade and is not important. The surface finish should not be too polished; a dull but smooth matt surface is best unless you are blueing the steel for cosmetic effects. The colors will, of course, run into each other if the work is heated from one end, and they should be viewed in a diffuse light to avoid specular reflections. The most usual difficulty is in deciding when to stop; the straw may appear to be too pale, and then, before you have time to think, becomes too dark. This is perhaps a stronger argument for slow and gentle heating than any that

has gone before! It does help to have a piece of cold steel alongside for comparison if the very palest straw is the aim. As soon as the color is "right" the piece must be quenched – in oil or water – to prevent any heat stored in the shank of the tool from taking it further. The quenching serves no purpose so far as the actual tempering is concerned.

The work can be heated in a blowlamp, using a VERY soft flame, but whenever possible I use a spirit lamp. It is very adequate for most sizes of tool, and though it takes longer than a gas burner this is all to the good. We are not in a hurry! It provides a very clean flame, and one which does not interfere with color formation. Even so, it is necessary to remove the work from the flame to observe the color, as it will not develop properly in the presence of burning fuel. Indeed, it is possible actually to remove the color with a reducing type of flame. Naturally, you must keep the work moving about in the flame in order to get even heating if you are tempering the whole.

Objects which are of irregular shape can be difficult. The heat should be applied to the heavy part of the section, and you must keep a very careful eye on things. Fine corners may "take off" into the blue before the main body has reached straw. For such work I always use the salt bath or domestic oven. But if you must use a flame, go very slowly indeed. The difficulty with the direct heating method is that we are applying the heat from the outside, and there can be no guarantee that the internal structure is up to the temperature; it certainly won't be if you heat too quickly.

If flame heating is the only means available, then you can try one of the "semi-direct" methods. One which is often recommended is to bring a fairly thick steel plate up to just below dull red

Tempering 47

and to expose the workpiece to the radiant heat, turning it about the while. The higher tempering temperatures may need the plate to be red-hot. You can do a similar thing with a firebrick oven; just arrange a few firebricks to form an open box, heat them with a torch, and then hold the work inside with tongs – again, turning it about all the time. Many use a sand-bath. A tray of dry sand is heated from below and the work either laid up on it or buried, the sand being turned aside to inspect the colors from time to time. (It helps to have a thin piece of similar material laid on the surface of the bed in that case, to act as an indicator). The sand must, of course, be kept well stirred while heating, to make sure that it is at an even temperature. I would not recommend sand for temperatures in the "Pale Straw" region, but for deeper colors it works well; as soon as you see a pale color you know that the others are not far behind.

Transmission Tempering This is the "classical" way for lathe tools, but it can be extended. The tool is heated at the shank end, and as this turns blue, so the purple – dark straw – straw – pale straw colors run toward the point. As soon as the pale straw reaches the region of the cutting edge the tool is quenched, point down, in water. The virtue of this method is, as I have already suggested, that the heat travels down inside the metal, and we can be fairly sure that the tempering has reached the center. The difficulty is that the temper is uneven, from point backward. In the case of a knife-tool there will be marked difference in hardness along the cutting edge, and a parting tool will get softer as it is reground. This is the main reason why I changed to the "two-stage" tempering process already described. Nevertheless, the method is sound, and if care is taken (very gentle heat, with the flame moved backward, away from the point, as the work gets hotter) satisfactory results can be assured.

The idea can be extended. Fig 21 shows a method of tempering a small milling cutter, of the type (used in horology) which is screwed on to an 8mm collet arbor. The copper rod is threaded and screwed into the cutter, and heated with a blowlamp. The heat runs down the rod, through the metal of the cutter, to the teeth. Note that the cutter is set on the rod as shown, so that the teeth are more or less of uniform distance from the hot rod. Fig 22 shows a similar device in use tempering a die. In this case the circular die is wedged into the end of a piece of copper tube, which has four slits in the end. There is a ball of steel wool inside the tube just below (but not touching) the die to prevent hot air currents from heating the center part. The tube transmits the heat to the die from the outer perimeter, and the whole is quenched when the cutting edges reach the right temperature. Again, the heating must be gentle. The

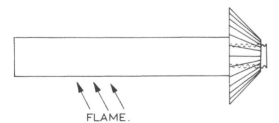

Fig. 21 Using a "heat pipe" when tempering a small dovetail milling cutter.

48 HARDENING, TEMPERING, AND HEAT TREATMENT FOR HOME MACHINISTS

Fig. 22 *Tempering a die. The copper tube acts as a heat pipe. There is a plug of steel wool within the tube to prevent heating by convection from below.*

advantage here is that the outside of the die (which acts more or less as a spring in service) is hotter than the cutting edge and so more deeply tempered – as it should be.

I doubt if many people make their own slitting saws these days, but similar objects can be tempered by gripping between two washers on a bolt, held by a nut. The heat is applied by heating the bolt. Many other examples will come to mind. The object is the same in all cases; first, to heat *from* the part of the tool which need not be hard, *toward* the cutting edge; and second, to arrange things so that where possible the heat travels through the interior of the tool, reaching the cutting edge from within.

Blazing Off. This is applicable mainly to work which has been oil quenched. As soon as it is removed from the quenching bath the tool or component is held over a small flame until the residual oil ignites and burns away. The heat so released (the work is taken from the torch or lamp flame) tempers the work. For larger pieces "the books" suggest binding some iron wire around, to hold more oil. The "theory" advanced is that the temper temperature is associated with the flash point of the oil. This is nonsense. The flashpoint is merely an indication of the temperature at which (under very artificial conditions) oil will *start* to ignite. The actual temperature reached will depend on the mass of the workpiece and the amount of oil retained, as well as on the heating value of the oil. For the experienced practitioner, and for very small clock parts like click-springs and pallets, the system works well, but they will have experimented a great deal and, most important, will "know their oil". Instructions in old books were the result of decades if not centuries of trial with one oil – from the sperm whale – but with the variety available and used today I would not care to give any instruction at all except to "Experiment first". It works very effectively, but does need experience.

To sum up; the ideal tempering medium is the salt or oil bath with the domestic oven or chip pan a practicable alternative. With these methods the exact temperature of the work is known, and conditions can be repeated exactly. The use of colors to judge the temperature is safe, but needs a little trial and experiment to judge the tints accurately; the temperatures will then be within the "tolerance" for the type of work we do. The actual degree of tempering needed should be considered, bearing in mind that most of the recommendations in Handbooks etc are for industrial conditions, not those of the model engineer. The temper heat should be held for a period – ideally for one hour per inch of section – and should be applied slowly. Tempering should be carried out as soon as possible after the initial quench. I will add just one

Tempering 49

final point; in some cases we do want a surface to be of maximum hardness and at the same time to have a fine grain – wearing and rubbing parts are cases. If this is so, then it is worth trying a temper at 100°C – just boil the part in water for half-an-hour or so. This will not reduce the hardness at all, but will achieve some grain refinement. For "fine grain" cutting tools I suggest a procedure on page 74.

CHAPTER 5

Heating Equipment

The Open Fire. There may be a few model engineers who own a blacksmith's hearth, and perhaps more who have inherited them from an earlier generation; it seems to have been an essential piece of equipment in the earlier times. I do have a small one with a hand-driven fan and though it is used mainly for smithy work, and then only rarely, I have hardened large objects in it. The last job was a pickaxe point, and I must confess that winding the handle got a bit wearisome! The forge was the natural thing to use – apart from saving expensive gas – as, of course, the point needed reforging as well.

Coke is the usual fuel – proper coke, not the soft stuff sold for domestic fires. As an alternative the egg-shaped manufactured fuel ("Phurnacite") is handy, as the eggs are more or less of uniform size. Housecoal is useless, and should not be used even to start the fire, and steam coal little better. For hardening you need a fairly deep fire, hot all through. To achieve this the fuel must be stirred about in the earlier stages. Once you have a nice glowing firebed the fan must be used with discretion – you need a *draft* rather than a "blast". The work is laid on top of the fire at first – in fact, it can be left there, preheating, while you bring the fire up. The piece is then set in the heart of the firebed, but where you can see it and observe the color. It must be turned about at intervals so that no one side is uppermost for any length of time. Take care that it is not exposed to the direct draft from the fan. Slow, even, heating is the order of the day, avoiding the impingement either of direct, cool, draft or a draft which has passed through any extra hot part of the fire. Overheating must be guarded against like the plague, and you must bear in mind that the metal will look cooler than it is until you get used to observing the color in contrast to the hot coke. You *can* bring a forge fire up to 1500°C and metal at 780°C will look dead cold in comparison.

A useful expedient is to use the semi-indirect method. Set a piece of (say) 2 inch steel pipe in the midst of the fire. Get this hot – a little above the temperature you need – and heat the work inside it. You are then able to judge the temperature more directly and, further, will be protecting the workpiece both from cold drafts and from local overheating. It is slower, but, as we have seen, fast heating is NOT the prime requirement.

Domestic Fires. This is a practical alternative to the smith's hearth for smaller pieces. After all, Nasmyth made the castings for his first steam engine in

Fig. 23 *A domestic stove of this type can be used to heat work for hardening.*

his *bedroom* fireplace! The ordinary open grate will get hot enough only for very small work, but any closed stove with a proper air control can be used for anything that will pass through the front firebars. (Fig 23) As with the forge, coke or "Phurnacite" can be used. I have had no experience using anthracite.

The grate must first be cleared of ash and clinker and the fire then built up by adding small quantities of fuel at a time until the firebed is as deep as can be accommodated. The aim must be to get a uniform rate of burning right through. Once this is achieved the front doors (or one of them) must be opened and the air valve in the ashpan adjusted to get the fire above, but not too much above, the temperature needed. The tool should be set in the upper part of the fire and, as in the case of the smith's hearth, should be turned about at intervals. You need have no fears that it won't get hot enough; the stove in Fig. 23 can be brought up to 1000°C very quickly indeed, and if you find any clinker in your grate, this is an indication that the grate temperature has, at some time, been of the order of 1300°C! The main problem I find is that unlike the smith's hearth you have no positive control; the response to adjustments of the air valve is slow, and you have to anticipate changes in the rate of burning.

Naturally, you must take account of your surroundings – it IS your hearthrug, after all! But the main objection I have to the use of the domestic stove for hardening is that the front grate-bars prevent the use of a piece of pipe. However, with the closed stove there is little problem in "Soaking"; once the fire has reached its temperature it tends to "stay put" for quite long enough for the size of work normally done. It is very useful for annealing, as the piece can be allowed to cool with the fire overnight. Even if the fire is not "out" in the morning this is not important. It will have cooled through the critical range very slowly and can be set in the ashpan to finish off.

Some books suggest that there may be a tendency toward both scaling and decarburisation when using the smith's hearth, but this need not cause us too much concern. It is true that a hearth with

52   HARDENING, TEMPERING, AND HEAT TREATMENT FOR HOME MACHINISTS

Fig. 23A *The author's hand fan-draft forge. Situated in an outhouse for safety, as the fire can throw out sparks to some height.*

fan blast can decarburise, but we are not dealing with the size of work normally done by the old blacksmith. You may need to take care if the heating time is half an hour or more, but it is only a case of avoiding direct impingement of the blast. Some scale will be formed, of course, but much less with the closed stove than you might imagine. The atmosphere *within* the firebed is mainly carbon monoxide and nitrogen – there is much less oxygen present than in a fan-driven fire. It is good practice, of course, to remove any scale which may be present from previous work, including the "mill scale" on black bar. More scale will be formed in the long heat associated with fire-annealing, and if the avoidance of scale is important the work should be protected. For overnight annealing a good way is to encase it in fireclay (NOT fire-cement) reinforced with iron wire. Or put it in a tin box packed with lime with a little charcoal mixed with it.

Blowlamps and torches. Most model engineers will have some form of paraffin or gas torch for use when brazing and it is natural that these should be the first resort when heating for hardening. I will deal with the various types in turn. I most strongly recommend that you NEVER, except in the most *dire* necessity, use Oxy-Acetylene (or Oxy-anything else) for any form of hardening operation unless the use of such equipment is part of your daily work. Even then it is risky. First, if the flame gets too close to the work, even for a second, that point will be overheated, decarburised, and almost certainly suffer from oxide penetration at the grain boundaries. Second, it is very difficult to get even heating as the heat source is so concentrated. If the flame is adjusted to avoid scaling there is then risk of *excess* carburisation which would result in cracking on quenching. Finally, it is a very expensive method of heating. Few people seem to appreciate that though the flame is very hot indeed the actual *heat output* is extremely low. In fact, the largest nozzle in the outfit I used to use (for welding ¼ inch steel plate) gave out much less heat than did my smallest paraffin blowlamp. It is a case of horses for courses; for its purpose oxy-acetylene torch does its work very well indeed, but that work is *not* heat treatment of steel unless you own a

Fig. 24 *Typical temperatures reached within the flame from a selfblown gas torch.*

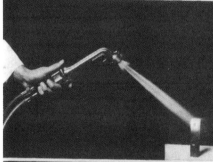

"Shorterising" surface hardening plant, and that is unlikely! So, let us turn our attention to the gas-air type.

The Torch Flame. Though I will be referring to "gas", the same remarks can be applied to the paraffin blowlamp flame. The difference in the fuel is not important – the heating value per pound mass of fuel (liquid or gas) is very nearly the same, and the paraffin (kerosene in USA) is vaporised before burning, so that the flame is in all essentials a gas flame. Such flames will appear as shown in Fig. 24, with a central cone surrounded by a more or less diffuse outer curtain, though its actual shape will depend on the fuel used, the type of air supply, and the air/fuel ratio. Primary combustion occurs within the inner cone and the heat release causes decomposition of the rest of the fuel gas. These fuel constituents burn in the outer envelope, using any excess air present within the flame and air drawn in from outside as well. The inner cone temperature will seldom exceed 1100°C but just beyond the tip of the inner cone the figure will be in excess of 1600°C. (The theoretical maximum is higher still, but is not reached because no burner is perfect and in any case there is considerable radiation of heat from the flame itself). Beyond this point the flame temperature diminishes again, as shown in the sketch. It is not always appreciated that a similar temperature gradient occurs

Fig. 25 *Gas torch with pressure air-supply, showing the range of flame formation possible. (Courtest Flamefast Ltd).*

Fig. 26 Two types of self-blown gas torch. The lower burner has the air-holes remote from the flame nozzle and can be used in confined spaces. That shown above needs a good supply of air around the flame. (Calor-Sievert Ltd.)

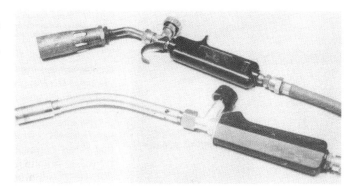

ACROSS the flame, but this is the case. If there is a long inner cone it may be that heating will be more efficient if the flame is laid *alongside* the work rather than be directed straight at it.

The general form of the flame will be the same for all fuels, perhaps some difference in color and some fuels will give a "sharper" cone than others, but there is considerable difference in CHARACTER of flame between those which come from a "self-blown" burner, such as those normally used on Propane or Butane, and those which have a separately controlled air supply derived from a fan or blower. There is some reasonably wide control of the *size* of the flame with the self-blown type, but any change in character (e.g., from "bushy" to "needle") requires a change in burner head. With the air-gas torch there is complete control of the flame, both as to size (within reason) and character solely by manipulating the air and gas control valves. There is no doubt that the burners with separate air and gas supply and control are by far the most efficient and convenient to use. The self-blown Propane brazing torch is, of course, very capable of the work and if you have the full range of burners will tackle all jobs from the largest to the smallest. But they do need careful attention both to gas pressure and to burner head selection. And they do need clear air around the burner head except for the special ones which have extension tubes beyond the air entrainment holes. When used in a firebrick "cave" the flame must have room to develop outside the entrance or it will "blow itself out". The paraffin (kerosene) blowlamp is much more flexible, largely because the fuel vapor is preheated, but also because the inflammability limit of paraffin is much wider than that of Butane, Propane and Methane (N.Sea Gas) so that the air/fuel ratio is much less critical.

All these flames will, if the burner size is right, exceed the temperature needed for heat treatment of steel. There is no problem here. However, we are concerned with even heating and, in most cases, with "economy". It is desirable that the flame be short and broad rather than one which, though equally "powerful" (in terms of heat release) is long and needle-like. With the air/gas type this requires only the manipulation of the controls but with the self-blown torch the burner head must be selected accordingly. Those described as "broad blowlamp" are usually the most appropriate.

Applying the flame. Heat transfer from

Fig. 27 *A crude but very effective heat conserving device. The hot gases escape between the back and top bricks. Note the little ceramic trivets for supporting the work.*

flame to workpiece is inadequate. On test, a piece of steel about the size of a 5/16 inch sq. lathe tool, laid flat on firebrick, took five minutes to bring up to the hardening temperature – something like 1500 units of heat from the burner transferring only 10 heat units to the steel. Not a very good score! By setting up a simple "cave" like that in Fig. 27 the heating time was reduced to 105 seconds; about 500 heat units. Not good, but better than before. You will, of course, quote my own words and say that the five minutes of the first example is much too fast for the heating-up time, and you would be right. But we have to HOLD the temperature for about another quarter of an hour and if this is to be done on the open firebrick the burner must be kept at full throttle the whole time. Using the "cave" it can be throttled down. Moreover, as the work will be heated largely by radiation from hot firebrick it will be heated more evenly.

And, finally, if we have several pieces to harden then we can save a considerable amount of gas. The "cave" is really a little furnace.

The intelligent use of firebrick will both save gas and ensure more even heating. I use three types. First, ordinary firebrick, from 1 to 3 inches thick. These are refractory rather than heat insulators – they will withstand very high temperatures. Second, lightweight "Insulating Bricks", of which "Fossalcil" and "Folsain" are typical. These look and feel like cork and are intended for heat insulation behind walls of firebrick in furnaces. They can be at 1000°C at one end and dead cold at the other, and are available in the same sizes as firebrick. Both firebrick and insulating bricks can be had from most hardware stores. The third type are "Hot Face" bricks – more refractory than the insulating type (which are friable and melt at around 1250°C) and with much better heat insulation than the ordinary firebrick. These seem to be available only from specialty suppliers (e.g., Messrs Flamefast Ltd, Pendlebury Trading Estate, Manchester M27 1FJ, or MPK Insulating Ltd, Hythe Works, Colchester CO2 8JU). They can be cut with a saw and drilled, and will stand reasonable loads. An accessory which I find most useful both upon open firebrick and in furnaces is the little ceramic "trivet" as used by enamellers – Fig. 28. I use these to support work so that flame can get beneath and, in furnace work, to ensure that the underside of the piece is radiation heated and not by conduction from the muffle.

Furnaces. The obvious next step from the cave is a suitable furnace. Those who do a

Fig. 28 *Method of holding a screwing die for quenching, with a trivet on which it is supported during heating on the right.*

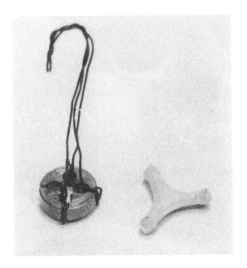

lot of brazing may well have one of the old "Utile" gas-fired forges which (in the days when I had access to town gas) served me as brazing hearth, heat treatment shop, and melting furnace. They are still available, modified for use on North Sea gas, from Alcosa Ltd (trading as William Allday & Co. Ltd, Stourport on Severn, DY13 9AP) but rather costly, I'm afraid. But for the serious practitioner, who needs heat for all the purposes mentioned above, they are, I believe, the best small general purpose heating unit available. The only drawback is the lack of temperature indication, but if you use heat sufficient to justify the cost of a Utile you will be pretty expert at colors anyway.

There are two small furnaces on the market which I know of which may be worth looking at. The first is simplicity indeed – the Alcosa "Export" Portable Forge. Fig. 29. Intended for use by itinerate farriers abroad, it can reach up to 1150°C and is very rapid in heating up. Once up to temperature the supply can be reduced – the full heat output is equivalent to about 16kw. There is no pyrometry and temperature must be judged by color. Very simple – almost crude – but cheap and effective. The second is the small gas-fired kiln as used by enamellers, marketed by the Flamefast Co. as their kiln type LN1000. This is rated to reach 850°C in 10 minutes or so, and will run up to 1000°C. It is equipped with a pyrometer and manually controlled firing rate, the maximum being equivalent to 3½kw. The chamber is about 7 in x 5 in x 7½ in and it can be fired on N.Sea gas, Propane, or Butane. Fig. 30.

There are others, of course, in varying degrees of sophistication and size. Anyone who practices the art of enamelling (or some types of pottery, for that matter) will have such a furnace which can usually be

Fig. 29 *The "Alcosa" portable propane fired furnace. The chamber is 9½ in wide x 5½ in high x 11½ in deep and can reach 1200° C with ease. (Courtesy William Allday Ltd).*

Heating Equipment 57

Fig. 30 The FLAMEFAST LN1000 kiln. This is intended for use by enamellers, but is more than adequate for heat treatment up to 1200°C. It is equipped with a pyrometer and is fired from either bottled or house supply gas. (Courtesy Flamefast Ltd).

used quite as well for heat treatment. There is also the implication that for model engineers, being the kind of ingenious people they are, it would not be difficult to "make your own". This is not as easy as it seems. There have been more fortunes lost (and eyebrows too!) over the combustion of gas than in most branches of engineering – it is not just a case of providing a jet and lighting the gas! It does need a lot of experiment, and I would suggest that it be done outdoors at first; delayed ignition associated with a chamber of a cubic foot or so can be more than interesting at times! But see Ch.IX.

Tube Furnace Most of my own work is done either in an old electric muffle or a salt bath, but I do make frequent use of a rigged up gas-fired tube furnace, shown in Fig. 31. The tube itself is a piece of 1½ inch exhaust pipe, relic of the days when I used "proper" (ie. "vintage") motor-cars, about 6 inches long. The tube is supported in 1 inch thick Folsain bricks with a hole cut using the ordinary tank hole cutter. One of the cores from the drilling is used to plug the back and as it has a hole from the pilot drill this enables me to set a homemade thermocouple inside if need be. The other core is used as a "front door". I give more details of the construction on page 90, but it IS very useful for those odd jobs which crop up which are neither large enough to warrant firing up the muffle, nor trivial enough to trust to direct heating.

Electric Muffles. There are many small electric muffle furnaces on the market, some for laboratory work, others for enamelling, and these provided the most economical heating device where any

Fig. 31 A very simple gas-fired tube furnace.

58 HARDENING, TEMPERING, AND HEAT TREATMENT FOR HOME MACHINISTS

Fig. 32 *The author's muffle furnace, recently equipped with a British Eurotherm 3-term electronic controller which allows it to be left unsupervised. The temperature is held to within 2°C.*

"soaking" is needed. They do take a fair time to heat up, but once at the operating temperature use very little power indeed. All are equipped with pyrometers these days, so that accurate temperature control is possible even if there is no thermostat. Heating is radiant into the work and it is easy to avoid scaling. Last but not least, they can be left to look after themselves with safety, making no noise and, if not thermostatically controlled there is usually a "thermal fuse" which breaks the circuit if the safe maximum is exceeded. My own (Fig. 32) was obtained second hand for the proverbial song some time ago, but even new ones are not prohibitively expensive – about the same cost as a gasfired one. Mine has a chamber 5 in wide × 4 in × 6in deep and is rated at 1000°C maximum, though most today go up to 1200°C.

Unlike the gas-fired type, it is relatively easy to make your own electric furnace so long as you take the normal precautions when dealing with lethal house voltages. Ready-wound muffles are available from such firms as Gallenkamps, Griffin & George, and other laboratory equipment suppliers (they are spare parts for their standard ranges of muffles) and these need no more than encasing in insulating materials and a metal or "Syndnyo" (or its equivalent) case. Heating elements are also available, either in the form of "Hot Rods" or "Heating Bricks" – refractory bricks with elements embedded in the face – or as refractory tubes with an element wound around. Home construction is dealt with in Chapter IX and the only point I would make is that you should seek the advice of the element suppliers early in the project. Fig. 33 shows a homemade furnace which is supplied in

Fig. 33 *The Kanthal Electroheat electric furnace. This is supplied as a kit for home construction. Note that an earthed shield has yet to be equipped over the terminals. One of the heating elements is seen in front of the furnace. (Courtesy Kanthal Ltd).*

Heating Equipment 59

"kit" form by Kanthal Electroheat, Inveralmond, Perth PH1 3EE, though as shown it does need guards fitting over the electrical connections.

Salt Baths. I have already referred to the salt-bath for tempering. Neutral and non-toxic salts are also available for the higher temperatures needed before quenching. They must not be confused with the ACTIVE salts used in cyanide hardening – the constituents of the neutral salts are no more than common salt (sodium chloride) mixed with a certain amount of potassium chloride to give the required thermal characteristics. The type which I use (Degussa GS660/WS720) melts at 670°C and can be used up to about 1000°C; it is obtainable from the same sources as the tempering salts. (p.45).

The salt is melted in a welded steel "pot". In industry these may be large and heated by gas or electricity – usually the former – but for the model engineer the vertical electrical tube furnace heating a pot made from steel tube is the most convenient. Gas heating presents certain problems (other than those already mentioned) and an electric heater is easier to control. The size of the pot depends on the work you want to do, of course, but that shown in Fig. 34 is very adequate. The actual pot is about 3 in. internal diameter and is 10 in. deep, with the salt bath itself about 7½ in. deep. (You must allow for the "tide to rise" when the work is put in!). It is, in fact, a small homemade laboratory furnace, and I give details of the construction later. It is, perhaps, larger than is really needed for model work but you need room for the essential pyrometer as well as the work.

For the initial melt the salt, which comes as a fine powder, is put in to about 4 inches below the top of the pot and, as this melts, more is very carefully added as the level sinks. When re-melting subsequently a fairly heavy iron lid should be set over the mouth, as a hard crust may form when the salt sets on cooling and there is just a risk of spitting. However, so long as the top end of the heating element lies above the salt level the crust should melt from the outside inward with no such trouble.

The workpiece should be preheated a little if it is likely to have water or oil in any holes, and if any holes are deep or large some consideration should be given to these, as there is a risk of spurting of hot salt as the air (or, worse, vapor) trapped in the hole expands. The piece can then be set in the bath, with a wire "handle" if need be. (A job like a file or scraper can, of course, have the tang protruding from the surface). The immersion of the work will

Fig. 34 *The author's laboratory type Austenising salt-pot furnace. Construction is described on page 98. Note that the "POISON" label refers to previous use with a cyanide hardening pot.*

temporarily reduce the bath temperature, but there is no need to adjust the controls – it should recover very quickly as there is considerable store of heat in the furnace. Once there the workpiece can be left for the prescribed time which, for a salt bath, can be HALF THAT NEEDED FOR A MUFFLE FURNACE; ie. 30 minutes per inch of thickness. This is one of the great advantages of the salt bath – the other being that the heating is bound to be uniform and to the correct temperature.

The work can be quenched in water, brine, or oil. Most of the adhering salt will "spall off" on quenching, in the first two, and the rest will dissolve. This will do no harm. Salt will, however, collect in the bottom of an oil bath and this must be sieved out at intervals. As I have said, the salt itself is quite harmless (when cold, that is; molten salt must be treated with the same respect as that accorded to molten metal – see Ch. 10.) and debris can be disposed of down the sink with a good flush of water. In which connection, the material DOES absorb water easily, and the salt powder should be kept in plastic bags in an airtight container. For the same reason, a lid should be kept on the pot when not in use.

Naturally such a pot should not be used for large tools. The salt level should not be less than three-quarters full nor should it rise more than an inch above the top of the heating element – and certainly should not approach the top of the pot. In one sense a larger diameter and shorter depth would help in this respect, but the cost of the tube and heating element then becomes very high. Safety precautions are dealt with in Ch. 10., but I will emphasize one point now. The liquid is HOT, as hot as molten brass, and you should be wearing suitable goggles, footwear, overalls and a cap. DON'T try to "rig up" a salt pot; it

must be properly constructed and be solid enough and heavy enough not to tip over, for the hot salt will set the floor on fire just as would hot metal.

Furnace Control. There is no method of control of a gas fired furnace which is reasonable in cost other than "manual". It *is* possible to obtain modulating flame burners with thermostats but the cost and complication would be difficult to justify for the model engineer. Electric furnaces can, however, be controlled automatically, in two ways. The easiest and cheapest is the "Energy Controller" – as is used on the hotplates of most electric cookers. This is, in effect, a simple time-switch. With the dial set at "0" the current is off all the time; set at "10" it is on all the time. In between the current is switched on and off in proportion – e.g., at "6" the current flows for 60% of the time, at "4" for 40%, and so on. This is very effective, and spare cooker controls (or even one from a scrap cooker) are usually rated at about 3kw, which is very adequate in most cases. The one essential is a pilot lamp, for it is all too easy to "forget" and leave it switched on all night. Again, cooker controllers have a set of contacts specially for such a lamp.

The proper "Thermostat" is far better, of course, as the temperature can then be controlled within close limits. The cost is greater, of course, as some form of relay or "solid state" switch is needed as well as the thermocouple. This latter CAN be the indicating thermocouple, but is usually a separate element. The cost and complication does depend, of course, on the degree of control needed. For the kind of heat treatment we are concerned with one which will hold the temperature to within +/– 8°C would serve and +/– 5°C is as close as is necessary; all steelmakers quote a temperature range for their products, usually 20°C wide.

Heating Equipment 61

Frankly, I have found that the only problem with my energy controller type is "forgetfulness"! I know pretty well where the dial has to be set for any particular temperature, but I have, on more than one occasion, been called away from the shop and forgotten to check the temperature before leaving.

Spirit Lamps. From the sublime to the ridiculous? By no means! The humble spirit lamp is invaluable and, I would say, essential when dealing with very small and delicate parts. It is cheap, it provides a very clean flame, and it needs no heavy gas bottles or trailing wires to feed it. My own is one of the little glass affairs with a round wick about inch diameter, but I do use one from a spirit fired model which has a larger, flat, wick from time to time. The glass one will bring the end of a 3/32 in. diameter rod up to quenching temperature quite happily. I have already referred to the use of a spirit lamp for tempering. For scriber points and even tiny boring tools the whole process can be carried out with this little fellow.

Handling. Naturally, you have to be able to hold the hot metal. I have already made passing reference to this from time to time. In many articles I have read the author has mentioned holding the work with "pliers". This does NOT refer to the normal mechanic's tool which, being (if of reasonable quality) hardened will soon lose their temper if so treated. The reference should be "Blacksmith's pliers" – the layman would call them "Tongs", perhaps! Fig 35 shows such a pair, and you will see that the nose has almost decorative curves. This is to give some slight spring in the holding. A ring like the link of a chain can be slipped over the handles to hold the nose closed on the work. Such pliers or tongs come in many shapes, but that shown is the most useful for heat treatment.

For smaller work the "laboratory tongs" shown in Fig 36 serve the same purpose. Usually made of stainless steel, they can be used to grip either with the ends or within the "ring". It is, however, important to obtain only the best quality; even these do occasionally tend to "cross their legs" and the cheaper variety (often sold for handling bacon in the frying pan) are useless. They can be obtained through

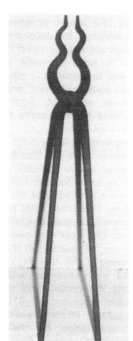

Fig. 35 *A pair of blacksmiths "pliers", about 18 inches long.*

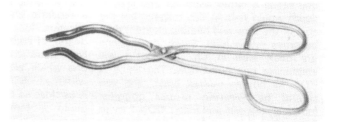

Fig. 36 *Laboratory tongs, about 8 inches tong, for smaller work.*

any reputable chemist, though they are unlikely to be held in stock. In all cases the nose of the tongs should be warmed before handling the metal, and on no account should they be wet, with either water or oil.

In situations where the use of "pliers" is not possible then iron wire can be bound around to make a handle or threaded through a hole if there is one. (See Fig. 28.) Remember that when the iron gets hot it both expands, which may loosen the hold, and loses strength. Take care that it is secure, and proportioned to the size of the job. At the same time, use wire that is the thinnest gauge that will be adequate, so that it will not interfere with the quenching action. There remains the case of the part which is so small that even thin wire would cause trouble. The answer here is to heat the work in a "boat" – just a piece of tube sawn in half – and to use a quench tank of such depth that no stirring is needed; the part will fall to the bottom at a rate which strips it of steam or vapor. The heat content of these tiny parts is so small that the quench is almost instantaneous anyway. They can be poured from the boat to the tank with no fears that the cooling will be too slow.

Conclusion. Domestic fires and the normal brazing torch equipment will cover most of the heating arrangements needed for the model engineer whose hardening program is "occasional". The same heat sources should cover the needs of annealing, and brazing torches are adequate for "open hearth" case-hardening referred to in Chapter 6. Those who make a lot of special tools, whose work involves the hardening of jigs and gauges, or who make a practice of hardening wearing parts on their models (as we all ought to do) will find that the simple electric or gas-fired muffle will help a great deal, and the salt-bath even more so. For tempering all but the simplest parts the low-temperature salt-bath is, as I have already indicated, far easier and more reliable than any other method.

In using brazing torches, however, it is essential to set brazing practice and brazing experience aside. You must "think of the atoms" as it were, all the time. The temperature is higher than is needed for silver-soldering and is more important. Further, you have to hold an even temperature for a very long time – just the opposite to brazing requirements, where long heating can cause problems and where we deliberately get one part hotter than the rest so that the alloy will "follow the heat". Naturally, it is impossible to cover every eventuality or every expedient in a chapter like this, but if you keep the "principles" outlined earlier always in mind you should have no difficulty in devising a satisfactory scheme for anything out of the ordinary.

CHAPTER 6

Casehardening

So far we have been concerned with work which needs to be hardened right through – tools, punches, chisels and the like – but there are many applications where SURFACE HARDNESS only is needed, the classic case being a crosshead pin. Such a component could, of course, be made from "Silver" steel, hardened, and then tempered to reduce the brittleness. However, the tempering would reduce the surface hardness and so the wear resistance – and we have had to use an expensive material. In "Casehardening" we take a low or medium carbon steel (in industry, perhaps an alloy steel) and modify the structure of the outer skin so that this can be hardened without unduly affecting the core. The main body of our pin will then have all the characteristics of the "mild" steel originally used but the surface is as hard as an untempered hardened high-carbon steel.

To bring this about we adopt a process known as "Carburising". You will recall the Chapter I that to make "Cast Steel" from wrought iron the metal was heated for a long period in the presence of carbon, so that the carbon content of the whole mass was increased. For case-hardening the process is similar, but the heating time is much less, with the result that the skin only of the metal takes up the carbon. Industrially the time is such that a casing of appreciable thickness – $1/16$ inch or more – will allow for subsequent grinding. For model-making such depths are unnecessary and we seldom resort to grinding anyway, though we may lap the surface to improve the finish. With thick cases there can be a dimensional change, but there is no need to worry about this for the depth of carburisation normal for model-making.

Once the part has been surface carburised it is heated again up to the hardening temperature and quenched. We CAN temper it if we wish, but this is not necessary and even if it is thought desirable to refine the grain a little, 100-140°C will suffice. However, we can modify the process and so derive one of the great advantages of casehardening over through hardening. We can machine the piece *after* carburising but *before* quenching. This will remove the case from the machined parts. Quenching will have no effect on the machined surfaces, and these will be soft. This is very normal practice, and many engine and machine parts are designed to be treated in this fashion. Fig. 37 is a case in point – a pin with a hardened bearing surface and two screw threads. If made from silver steel these threads would be dead hard unless

64 HARDENING, TEMPERING, AND HEAT TREATMENT FOR HOME MACHINISTS

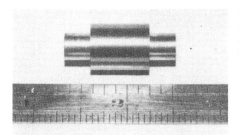

Fig. 37a Piece of M.S. prepared for carburising. 37b; After carburising, one end screwed and the other plain turned. 37c, The same piece after reheating and quenching. 37 d; The plain end has been screwcut and the whole cleaned up. The bearing surface is dead hard, but both screwed ends are soft.

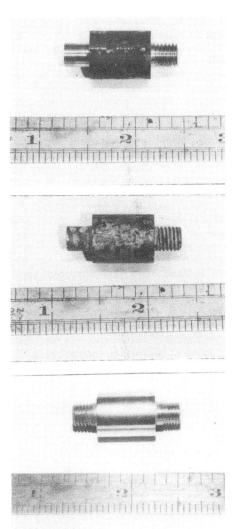

tempered, yet if they were tempered to the safe hardness the wear resistance of the pin will be reduced, perhaps unacceptably. The pin shown is, in fact, made of casehardened mild steel. At "a" the pin is rough machined at the ends, about 1/16 inch oversize, but the bearing surface is finished. At "b" it has been carburised all over and then the case turned away from the ends, down to finish size. One thread has been screwcut. At "c" the pin is seen after reheating and quenching – anti-scale paint was used. Finally, at "d" you see the thread cut on the other end (after quenching) and the whole cleaned up and polished. BOTH threads are soft, despite the fact that one was cut before and the other after quenching, yet the bearing surface is dead hard, and took the teeth off the file. The hard skin was subsequently measured and found to be between 0.003 and 0.005 inch thick.

There are other situations where casehardening can be used to advantage. For example, a complex form-tool can be made from mild steel and carburised. After hardening it will have a surface harder than tempered carbon steel. It will not stand regrinding, but the tool life will be slightly longer and if it is to be used only the once we have saved a lot of expensive material. Made from carbon steel a pivot pin or a lathe center will need to be tempered; casehardened – there is no need, and the wear resistance will be

Casehardening 65

greater. In ANY situation where the part is subject to shock loading or where toughness is needed for other reasons, but at the same time resistance to wear is required, casehardening is the answer; you have the load bearing core in a state to take the stress, and the surface conditioned to resist wear.

Carburising. There are three main methods in use, one of which, the active salt-bath, is not suitable for model engineer's uses as it involves molten cyanide salts, which are lethally poisonous. In industry the next most common method is BOX CARBURISING. This involves the setting of the work in a heavy welded steel box filled with a carburising material. The lids are sealed or "luted" with fireclay. The compound used is specially formulated; largely charcoal, but with additives to increase its effectiveness. Heating times are of the order of six hours or so. For our small parts nothing so elaborate is needed. I have used sturdy tin boxes – they last for two or three heats – or a piece of steel pipe (not galvanised) with one end equipped with a screwed plug and the other sealed with fireclay. (Note, fireCLAY, not firecement, which will set hard; obtainable from most hardware stores). The carburising element is charcoal, but this, by itself, is slow acting. An "Activator" must be added and Sodium Carbonate (not Bicarbonate) is the most easily obtainable. Add about 1% by weight to the charcoal and mix it thoroughly. Alternatively you can add some of the "Open Hearth" compound, "Kasenit No. 1", which I will be mentioning later. About 5% will suffice. Other materials can be used – I have successfully casehardened using old leather bootlaces wrapped around the metal, for example! Presumably the tanning process provided an activator!

The work must be completely surrounded by the compound, which should be packed down hard. The lid must be sealed against ingress of air. It is then heated to between 880°C and 920°C for a length of time which is determined by the depth of case required. The first hour will penetrate about 0.008 inch and a case depth of 1/16 inch may be reached after seven hours. (This assumes we are casing mild steel). For model engineer's work a depth of 0.008 inch should be adequate, and a one-hour heat will be long enough; any greater depth of case may enforce a subsequent grinding operation. Note that these times are times AT the carburising temperature, and you must allow some extra for bringing up the temperature.

The box is allowed to cool, and this can be outside the furnace if no subsequent machining is required. The parts can then be taken out – and here it is worth suggesting the inclusion of a blank test

Fig. 38 *This case-hardened pin has had a flat ground on the side and has then been etched to show the hardened case.*

66 HARDENING, TEMPERING, AND HEAT TREATMENT FOR HOME MACHINISTS

piece. This can be reheated and quenched to check that sufficient hardness has been reached. I use a piece of round bar and grind off the side to form a flat after quenching. This is etched with 25% nitric acid in water and, as seen in Fig. 38, the depth of case is very visible. This is, of course, magnified by the "circularity" of the specimen; the actual thickness CAN be calculated if you like, but I am, as a rule, content if the test shows the case to be "adequate!" Any "part-machining" can now be done.

We next have to harden the case, but occasionally a further operation may be desirable. We have held the metal well above its critical temperature for very a while – longer than we might for heat treating a carbon steel. This may have caused some coarsening of the grain. This will not be serious if the time is an hour or less, but if longer it can be worth attending to. If the box was heated for 3 hours or more I would always refine the grain size before hardening. This refining is done by heating to a temperature which depends on the carbon content of the original steel as under:

% Carbon	0.1	0.2	0.3	0.4
Temperature °C	910	890	870	860

Heat for the regular "one hour per inch of thickness" and then quench in oil at about 30°C. This is NOT a hardening process, but solely directed to reducing the grain size of the core. In fact, with very mild steel (below 0.1% carbon) air cooling will suffice and there is no need to quench.

The component is then brought up to 760-780°C. The heating time is short, as we are concerned only with the case; a few minutes is enough, and the work is then water-quenched. I have already remarked on the need for tempering.

Frankly, this is totally unnecessary for cases of the thickness we need – and seldom for thicker ones – but it is found sometimes that surface crazing appears during the grinding operation, and normal practice is to temper at about 150°C if experience shows that this is likely.

Open-hearth Carburising. Closed box carburising is seldom needed for model work, and even less often used, if only because it requires the use of a muffle. Though it can be done by setting the box in an open fire; I have done this, and it is very effective, as the temperatures at this stage are not all that critical. However, surface hardening on the smith's hearth has been used for well over a century, and is more than adequate for thin cases. In this process the metal is brought up to about 800°C (between 780 and 850) – usually referred to as "bright red". The part is then covered with a special compound, either by dipping or by rolling it about, until the surface requiring hardening is completely covered. The compound in contact with the metal melts, and carbon is absorbed. The process can be repeated several times if a thicker case is needed. (A single "dip" provides perhaps 0.002 to 0.003 inch). The compound I have used for 50-odd years is Kasenit No. 1, and it is readily obtainable from model suppliers and even from good ironmongers.

Some practitioners quench immediately if no intermediate machining is needed, but I prefer to reheat to between 760 and 800°C. I always use plain water, though brine is permissible. No grain refining is needed. The resulting case will be very hard – some would say it is harder than with box carburising, but is very thin. I seldom use less than two applications and often three or four, but I have yet to find a case which was not thick enough for the purpose intended.

Casehardening 67

Naturally, if intermediate machining is required it is necessary to allow the work to cool. This can be allowed in air, but I usually clap a piece of firebrick on top to reduce the rate slightly. It is not critical at all; indeed, there is little that is critical about the whole process though naturally the more carefully the temperatures are observed the better the results. An occasional problem is scaling. However, we are dealing with a MILD (or at most, medium carbon) steel and there is no need in this case to heat slowly. When carburising it is only the skin that is affected anyway. It is not possible to use anti-scale paint, nor a salt-bath, but fortunately the compound itself does have anti-scale properties. It is, of course, only prudent to remove any existing scale from black bar (if one needs to harden such) before starting. There is, of course, no reason why you should not heat the metal in a little box surrounded by the compound. I have done this occasionally, when I have a number of very small parts to deal with at once. It saves time. You do have to be sure that the contents are up to temperature, of course, and you should use a "thin" (shallow) box for that reason. But such a procedure does ruin the innate simplicity of open-hearth carburising, and you are unlikely to get *better* results by using a box. It is, occasionally, more convenient, that is all.

Now and then there may be difficulties in applying the compound – on a ratchet wheel, for example – to be sure that it works on the desired faces. The compound can be wetted with water and applied as a paste. It is then heated very gently to dry out, after which the procedure is as described above. There are situations where secondary machining might be needed with box carburising but can be avoided with the open hearth method. A screw thread, for example, can

be protected from the action of the compound by wrapping wire or shim steel around it. Tapped holes can be plugged with a screw, and plain holes by inserting plugs. And, of course, if all you need to harden is the face of a tappet or the end of a tool it is easy enough to devise means to restrict the application of compound only to that particular spot.

Steels for casehardening. Any "straight" carbon steel can be carburised – you can, if circumstances require it, carburise silver steel! As a rule, however, the process is normally applied to the low-carbon "mild" steels or, at most, to those with carbon contents below 0.3%. Free-cutting steels can occasionally present problems – the inclusions which provide the free-cutting qualities *may* cause surface crazing. I would not advise box carburising these materials, but have successfully surface hardened them by the open-hearth method. Steels specifically designed for (box) casehardening are available. These usually contain about 1% of Nickel, the object being to reduce the grain growth during the prolonged heating. Straight carbon steels intended specifically for casehardening by either process are En 32C (080M 15 in BS970/1972) which is 0.15% carbon, 0.8% manganese, and En 21 (130M15) which is 0.15% carbon 1.3% manganese; somewhat stronger at 40 ton/sq.in tensile strength.

Alloy steels should not be casehardened without detailed heat treatment specifications from the makers. All such steels are "heat treatable" and you may well set up adverse conditions during the carburising process if you do not get the temperature right. Never try to caseharden scrap steel, or offcuts from the machine-shop skip. They may be anything, from low grade steel for making decorative handrails to chrome-nickel-molybdenum-titanium alloy! On the other hand, wrought iron (easily identifiable by the spark test) casehardens beautifully, and you CAN caseharden cast iron! Obviously you must have regard to the shape of the casting – complex outlines may crack in the quench, but hardening the end of a plunger or even a valve-rocker presents no problems.

Examples. Fig. 39 shows a few examples. Top left is a ball-joint made to replace the carburettor control on an ancient motor-car. Bright drawn hexagon bar was used and finish machined completely before hardening. The thread was protected with thin iron wire and whitening, and only the ball end was dipped in Kasenit No. 1. It was quenched directly after the second application. Center top is the crankshaft for a model steam engine (the "Williamson") with a hardened crankpin. In this case the bearing surface was finished to dimension, but the stem which fits into the web was left 1/32 inch oversize. The workpiece was not parted off from the stock at this stage. The bearing was given the Kasenit treatment twice, being dipped into the compound only sufficiently to cover it. After cooling slowly the rest of the machining was completed and parted off, after which the flanged end was finished. It was then reheated and quenched. There was no difficulty at all in riveting the spigot on assembly.

Top right is a different situation. This is a tap needed for finishing the internal threads of the boxwood chucks used on my Holtzapffel lathe. The cost of a length of silver steel this size would be prohibitive for the amount of work it has to do. Further, there would have been some risk of cracking even if great care were taken, as the threads have sharp roots and a fine angle of 50°. It was made of *black* mild steel (ie. hot rolled, not bright drawn) so that there was no need to normalize it first. It was given a single treatment with Kasenit No. 1 and quenched directly. The cutting edges were very lightly stoned afterward. It has served its purpose with no difficulties.

Bottom left is a drilling jig for some cylinder covers and the associated cylinders, the number going through the shop justifying the use of jigs. It was made from Bright Drawn steel which was first normalized before machining. It was

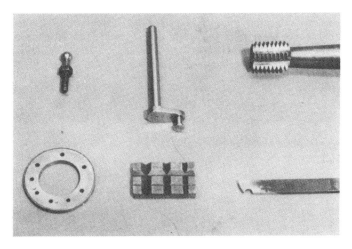

Fig. 39 *Casehardening. L to R, top. Pivot pin; engine crank; large special tap. Bottom; drilling jig; vee jaw for machine vise; special formtool.*

Casehardening 69

carburised for 30 minutes in a tobacco can using a mixture of charcoal and Kasenit No. 1 compound. This was done to ensure that the inner surface of the holes was hardened. Bottom center is the grooved jaw for a drilling vise, which was casehardened "open hearth", the part being laid, face down, in a tray of compound. Three doses were applied. There was a little scaling on the back, and just a very little distortion. It would have been wiser to normalize it before machining (BDMS was used) but the fault was not sufficient to warrant the making of another.

Bottom right is an example of a special form tool. This was made from mild steel for no other reason than that I had no high-carbon of the right size and only a limited stock of a size which could be machined down. This was given doses of Kasenit No. 1, allowed to cool, and then reheated and quenched. The compound was applied only to the tool tip. The result was outstanding. The case was thick enough to permit light stoning of the top face to give a sharp edge, and the performance (ornamentally turning gritty hardwoods) surprising. As no tempering was needed the cutting edge was harder than could have been obtained with a conven-

tional tool steel. And contrary to supposition, such tools have a harder time turning these exotic woods than when turning most metals, for the only route for the escape of the heat is through the tool – and, of course, no coolant can be used.

Conclusion. Casehardening is *not* a substitute for through hardening with a high carbon steel, but a process which earns its place from its very nature. We can design a component in material which provides the strength, fatigue resistance, or other property needed and then surface harden it to give the required wear resistance. The nature of the process is such that selective hardening can readily be applied, and the risk of cracking is very much reduced. Use of the open hearth method gives very adequate thickness of case for our purposes and is much quicker than through hardening, with the need for subsequent tempering adding to the time taken. At the same time, casehardening *can* be used for such things as lathe tools etc. if circumstances demand. One final point is worth making. There is often no real need to harden a rubbing surface, but if it IS hardened and polished the friction loss will be reduced. The almost glass hard surface produced by casehardening is a real advantage in all such applications.

CHAPTER 7

Other Heat Treatment Processes

(1) Annealing, Normalising, and Stress Relieving. These three processes are often confused. They are carried out in similar ways, but the three purposes are different. *Annealing* is the softening of steel previously hardened, whether by heat treatment or by cold working. *Normalising* is a process where the internal structure of the steel is restored to "normal" after some previous operation – say forging. *Stress Relief* is, as its name implies, the release of stresses which may have been locked up in the steel, either by heat treatment or by cold forming. "Tempering" is a special form of stress relieving. We will deal with these processes in turn.

Annealing. The steel will be Martensitic in structure and it is necessary to change this to one containing pearlite and either ferrite or cementite, as it would have been had the steel been cooled slowly from the initial austenitic state. This means that we must first bring it to a temperature high enough to ensure that the steel is above the transformation temperature, and then cool it at a rate that will allow the transformation to pearlite.

In the case of low carbon and medium carbon steels (below 0.85%) this will be about 30°C above the upper critical, but for higher carbon content a temperature somewhat above the *lower* critical will suffice. The recommended figures are given in the table below. (See also Fig. 41). In each case the higher temperature relates to the lower carbon content. None is critical to within ± 10°C.

The metal must be heated slowly and then "soaked" at the annealing temperature for one hour per inch of thickness – in the case of rectangular sections the smaller dimension is taken. It should then be cooled as slowly as can be contrived. If heated in a muffle with a good heat insulation to the chamber it may be allowed to cool down in the furnace. Otherwise it must be set in *hot* ashes or some similar material which will retain the heat. Thin, flat, sections can be cooled between two preheated insulating bricks. The higher the carbon content the more important is the slow rate of cooling. For "mild" steel the piece may be cooled in air once it has dropped to around

Carbon, %	Below 0.1	0.1-0.3	0.3-0.5	0.5-0.7	0.7-0.9	Above 0.9	"Silver Steel"
Temp.°C	920-900	870-830	850-800	820-780	800-780	790-760	770°C

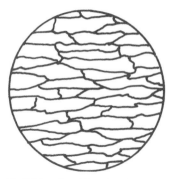

Fig. 40 *Elongation of the grains of steel caused by mechanical forming processes.*

400°C, but it is inadvisable to quench it even from a low temperature. Note that work *must* be fully preheated before immersing in a salt-bath for annealing.

Annealing *high speed steel* is a chancy business for the amateur, especially as any subsequent hardening may well be beyond the capabilities of the equipment available. However, if such an operation *must* be carried out the piece should be heated VERY slowly to 850°C, held there for one hour per HALF-inch of section, and cooled very slowly indeed; a muffle furnace is almost essential, and the cooling can be best effected by progressively reducing the power input until it has fallen to around 550°C before turning it off completely.

Normalising. After forging or rolling a metal the natural shape of the "grains' will be distorted – see Fig. 40. The situation may be even worse if some of the forging or, e.g., bending has been done at below the proper forging temperatures or when the steel is bright-drawn. To reform and refine the grain structure it is again necessary to reheat to above the critical temperatures but to a much higher degree than is needed for annealing, especially for the high carbon steels.

These must be taken right up into the full austenitic region. Fortunately tool steels seldom require normalising, which is needed chiefly to improve the machineability of medium and low carbon (and alloy) steels. The following table shows recommended temperatures.

Carbon %	0.1	0.2	0.3	0.4	0.6
Temp, °C	920	900	880	860	840
	0.8	1.0	1.1	1.2	
	820	830	900	925	

10°C up or down from these temperatures will serve. The temperature must be maintained, as in the case of annealing, for one hour per inch of section, and the cooling must, again, be slow.

Fig. 41 shows the annealing and normalising range on the iron-carbon diagram. **Stress Relief.** Certain manufacturing processes induce considerable stresses within the metal, in particular cold drawing and welding. The former sets the surface skin under compression and there may be a locked-up tensile stress in the core. The result is that when any part of the surface is removed symmetry is lost and the shape will distort. In welding, part of the metal is brought up to very high temperatures indeed and differential contraction between this and the cold or relative cold parts can induce stresses – often sufficient to distort during the actual welding. The degree of stress relief needed is different in the two cases. Cold drawn or cold rolled steel may be relieved sufficiently to prevent distortion during machining by heating to between 400°C and 500°C and allowing the part to cool in air. It is important that you ensure even heating, otherwise the last state may be worse than the first due to thermal expansion differences. For welded components

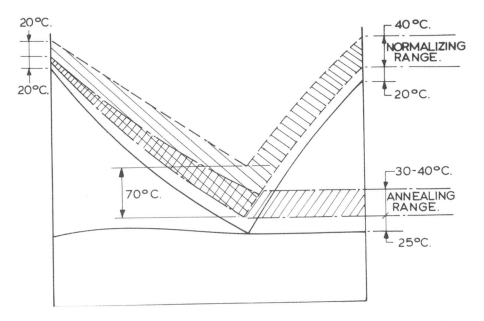

Fig. 41 Approximate annealing and normalising temperature ranges superimposed on the iron-carbon equilibrium diagram. This can be used in conjunction with fig. 13 if no definite data are available.

(I am referring to the small parts used in models, not to homemade bridges or radio masts!) it is best to give a full anneal as the condition in the vicinity of the weld is unknown.

Parts which have been heat treated will, of course, be under considerable intercrystalline strain – this is part of the hardening process. The subsequent tempering process is a form of stress relief, even though in this case we also aim at some controlled transformation as well.

(1) Scaling. In all the above processes some surface scaling is to be expected, and this can be a nuisance. It can be prevented by the use of anti-scale paint, binding with wire and encasing in whiting, or by the use of charcoal in the muffle if the latter is used. However, for small parts an ingenious method is described in some early books. The parts to be heated are set in a box filled with slaked lime ("builder's lime") mixed with up to 5% of charcoal. The latter absorbs any oxygen present, but is not sufficient to cause any carburising. Another such recipe suggests the use of fine cast-iron turnings as the packing medium. The former method does work, but the heat insulating properties of the lime enforce a long heating time.

(2) Rehardening. In the course of time tools may be reground so far that the tip is brought back into the more deeply tempered region. This applies especially to woodworking tools, but cold chisels and scrapers suffer in the same way and it can apply to sliderest tools as well. When this happens there is no option but to reharden. It might be thought that it would be necessary only to reheat, quench, and temper again. This is well enough with "coarse" tools made from relatively low carbon steel; I treat my pickaxe, wrecking bar, and similar tools in that way. But if you try to reharden a high-carbon steel tool in this fashion the results will, at best, be disappointing and you may find that the tool cracks. We must restore the metal to the condition it was before the initial hardening process was carried out, and this means that it should be fully annealed first. I have already dealt with the process and there is no need to repeat it. However, I can add a refinement. If the tool of some importance is to be rehardened it will pay to retemper to about 300°C before commencing the annealing process. This will effect an almost complete stress relief to the structure and I have never had a tool crack when this procedure has been followed. I recommend it strongly for those tools where there is considerable difference between the temper in the shank and in the point. It is only necessary to heat up very gently to "blue", allow it to cool just a little, and then to proceed with the full annealing heat.

(3) Hardening Ornamental Tools. The "Ornamental" turner has a problem not met with in most other types of turning. The art comprises the cutting of fairly deep patterns on the surface of work previously turned by normal methods to an acceptable shape. The final effect depends entirely on the reflection of light from the multitude of facets so formed – and with well executed work almost dazzling reflections can be seen on a woo

d like Ebony. His problem is twofold. First, there is NO means whereby the incised decoration can be polished. The surface must be reflective with "tool finish". This surface finish can never be better than the finish on the tool, and for this reason the sharpening of the tool is taken to what might appear to be extreme limits. After forming with normal grinding methods and a fine India stone the surface is "rough polished" using hard Arkansas stone, the tool being held in a special jig (the "Goniostat") which ensures that both the cutting angle and the "pattern angle" are accurately formed. It is then lapped using the finest oilstone dust on a brass lap, and finally polished (still using the goniostat) on an iron lap with jewelers rouge. The problem is that modern tool steels will not give the refined grain size which was normal with the steel used when the art was being developed, and the common complaint is that "the steel won't take the polish".

The second difficulty is that such a tool may have to make three or four hundred "cuts" each at a different setting of the apparatus. It is impossible to remove it for sharpening once the process has started. As previously mentioned, the only route by which the heat of cutting can escape is through the tool; the workpieces are very good heat insulators. This means that the tool must remain sharp and, hence, hard over a long period – and any loss of sharpness can be fatal to the effectiveness of the work. These two requirements, finest grain size and maximum hardness, cannot be achieved with the normal carbon tool steels (and even less so with high-speed steel). It IS possible to achieve the hardness required by using a file steel. After annealing at about 770°C (and on no account above 790°C) the tool can be hardened from 760°C/780°C and quenched in brine. The subsequent tempering should be as mild as possible at the point – I do no more than boil in water for half an hour for cutting frame tools, but sliderest tools must be tempered at least to straw in the shank.

Alternatively, with "Silver Steel" a grain refining process can be carried out, and this will give very satisfactory – results even if the purists will say "Still not as good as a genuine Holtzapffel"!

After machining the piece to the required section and rough forming the necked end (if any) heat to between 820°C and 850°C for one hour per inch of section. In the case of tools with the $\frac{9}{16}$ inch square shanks the "ruling section" is the inch or so behind the point. Quench in oil at about 20-25°C. The working end may now be ground – carefully – almost to finish size, but in the case of the heavy sliderest tools $\frac{1}{32}$ inch should be left on. Reheat slowly again, but to 760-770°C only, and quench in brine at 15-20°C. Temper immediately to not more than 150°C for at least 30 minutes, and then "let down" the shank of sliderest tools with the actual cutting point kept cool in water. At this temper very little, if any, of the hardness will be lost, but the hardening stresses will have been relieved. The metal will have a very fine grain and be as hard as possible.

(4) Heat Treatment of Medium Carbon Steel. So far we have been considering the "hardening" of steel to make cutting tools and the like, but there are many other cases where some form of heat treatment will improve the quality of the material in other directions. Indeed, by far the greatest amount of heat treatment in industry is directed to this end.

If you refer back to Fig. 13 (and, perhaps, refresh your memory from the associated text!) you will see that (say) 0.4 carbon steel under normal (ie. slowly cooled) conditions consists of grains of pearlite surrounded by ferrite; a tough material set in a matrix of soft material. The resulting steel is fairly tough and strong – "better" (for some purposes) than mild steel. Suppose, now that we were to quench this steel from a high temperature? There is insufficient carbon present for total transformation into the form of iron carbide we know as Martensite, so that the structure will, in effect, be that of hard Martensite "diluted" with ferrite, It will possess some of the character of a high-carbon steel (hardness and toughness) and some of those associated with "mild" or low-carbon steel; ductility and softness. Further, we can temper the steel. This has a considerable effect, as in the case of high carbon steel, and in this case the selection of the best temperature is the most important part of the treatment. The mixture of tempered Martensite and ferrite crystals can be adjusted to give higher strength, high yield point, better impact resistance, and so on. Fig. 41 shows the effect on a typical 0.4% carbon steel, and you will notice that there is a dip in the Impact resistance (Izod Impact Test) in the middle tempering range. This need not worry you too much, as it is still considerably higher than that of the unheat-treated steel.

To give an example, let us consider our old friend EN8. (080M40 in the BS 970 1972 nomenclature) In the normalized condition typical properties would be 38 T/sq.in. UTS; 27 T/sq.in Yield; Elongation (ductility) 28% and an Izod impact resistance figure of 15-17 ft.lb. The metal is Austenised by heating to 830-860°C for 1 hour/inch, and then quenched in oil. The tempering temperature must then be selected according to the properties we need. For maximum toughness and the most arduous fatigue and shock loading conditions this would be between 550

Other Heat Treatment Processes 75

and 650°C and then air cooled. (Note that tempering salt will not operate at this figure and the work must be done in a muffle). At 600°C the UTS would be around 42 T/sq.in, Yield point about 28 T/sq.in, Elongation perhaps 29% – not a great change. But the impact resistance has gone up to 80 ft.lb – around four times as great as before. The fatigue resistance also will be improved. If we tempered at 400°C we would raise the UTS to about 50 T/sq.in, but both ductility and shock resistance would be less – though still better than that of the normalized steel.

For completion, the normalising temperature is 840-860°C, but if you have EN8 which is bright drawn from the Oil Hardened and Tempered condition (O.H.&T. in the supplier's list) it is, in fact, in about its toughest condition, with a yield point of around 46T/sq.in. and an Izod figure of about 60. You are not likely to better this. However, most EN8 is supplied to model engineers in the bright drawn state with no heat treatment, and normalising may be prudent before working on it.

Fig. 42 *The influence of tempering temperatures on the properties of a typical 0.4% carbon steel after oil quenching from about 850°C.*

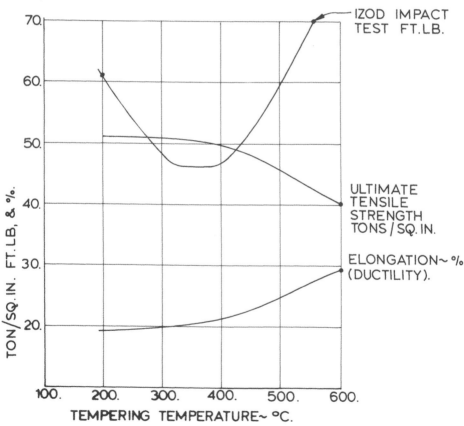

76 HARDENING, TEMPERING, AND HEAT TREATMENT FOR HOME MACHINISTS

Similar treatment can be carried out on almost all steel with a carbon content above 0.2%. But it is MOST important that you know exactly what material you are treating *and* what treatment to give it. Unfortunately most firms now send their work out to specialists and published data is hard to come by. If the steel can be identified with an "SAE number" (Society of Automotive Engineers, USA) then either the SAE "Handbook" or 'Machinery's Handbook" can give some guidance. The problem for the model engineer is in selecting the required tempering temperature. It is on this, rather than the initial quench, that the final properties depend, and if a *range* of tempering temperatures is offered this presents a puzzle. Perhaps you might think it safe to work at the midpoint of the range, but in the absence of specific data you cannot be sure of what properties you are improving. So, for *any* heat treatment of medium carbon or alloy steel it is best either to do nothing, or to go to the fountain head. The makers of the steel can give you chapter and verse, and if you give the British Steel Corporation the specification number and the application you have in mind they should be able to provide you with detailed figures both for initial heat and for tempering. It is fortunate that most of our work does not need high tensile or high impact values – and I hope that the data I have given for our old friend EN8 will help where something better than "BDMS" is needed.

I should, perhaps, add a final note. The old BS970/1955, with its "EN"* numbers, was replaced in 1972 with a new, and far more logical, specification reference. (The number itself, in most cases, tells us the carbon content). Details are given in "Model Engineer's

(* E.N. means Engineering Number)

Handbook" and in App.3, and I would strongly recommend that you start using these new numbers – not least because steel is just not being made to some of the old EN numbers any more. (This includes a favorite of mine – 3% Nickel steel EN21!) The "new" British Specification has been in use now for over 10 years, after all.

(5) Coil Springs. We make the majority of our coil springs from wire which is already hardened and tempered. The act of coiling them around the mandrel stresses these beyond the elastic limit (the spring-maker's term for this is "scragging"!) and this actually improves the strength of the material. However, there are occasions when this is just not possible the gauge – of wire is too thick for the diameter of the mandrel. In these circumstances it is necessary to soften (anneal) the wire, wind the spring, and then harden and temper again. Unfortunately we seldom have details of the steel of which the wire is made. It may lie between 1.0% carbon, 0.4% manganese, and 0.7% carbon, 0.8% manganese. It should be annealed at about 780°C; this is not critical, but the small mass of the wire does mean that some care must be taken over the cooling. This wire can air-cool fast enough to reharden. The spring can then be wound, and I suggest that you allow either for subsequent stretching or compression to "scrag" the spring after heat treatment. Close-coil the ends and either flatten them on the grinder or form the loop, as required, at this stage.

Directly hardening with a flame is most unwise. There is risk of getting some part too hot and it is impossible to be sure of even heating. Set the spring or springs inside a steel or copper tube and heat this to 780°C from the outside as evenly as you can. The springs can then be poured into the oil-bath – there is no need to

Other Heat Treatment Processes 77

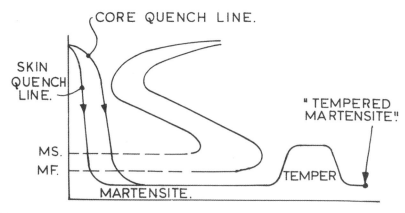

Fig. 43 *Idealized diagram of the normal "Hot Quench and Temper" hardening process. There is considerable thermal shock as the metal passes through the "MS" to "MF" range when Martensite is being formed.*

agitate for so small a mass of metal and the spring falling to the bottom will be sufficient. You must now be very careful, for at this stage the spring will be very brittle indeed – I have known fine ones even break under their own weight.

The tempering does present difficulties. It is almost impossible to use the "color" indication, as any attempt to polish the spring may result in breakage. The required temperature is very high – 300-310°C – well above the limit either for the domestic oven or for boiling in oil. "Blazing off", referred to earlier, is frequently resorted to. With experience (or prior experiment) it is effective, but let me repeat that the flash-point (or even the fire point) of the oil has nothing to do with the tempering temperature; this depends entirely on how much oil is retained on the spring. If there is not enough to bring the wire up to 300°C then the process must be repeated, and repeated immediately. Only a trial can tell whether it is necessary. However, it does work, and the procedure is to extract the spring from the quenching oil and then hold it in the flame of the spirit lamp until the oil ignites; as soon as it does so move it further from the spirit flame and allow the oil to burn away. Quench in oil when the flame goes out and then repeat if necessary, as it almost certainly will be for heavy gauge wire. It is almost essential to make a trial spring if this procedure is to be adopted.

The salt bath is the ideal method, of course. This gives absolute control and if a little wire "spray" – like an umbrella upside down which has lost its cover – is made a number of springs can be tempered at once. There is no need to quench from the salt bath, but once the spring has cooled somewhat it can be immersed in hot water to remove the salt adhering to it.

An alternative is the sand-bath, a process which can be very effective for leaf springs. The bed should be fairly deep and kept turned about as it is heated. A test piece of similar bright steel is set on the sand (a piece of the same spring material is best) and as soon as the temper color appears on this the springs can be arranged in the bed and hot sand heaped over, the heating lamp or torch being removed at the same time. Sand is not a very good conductor, so that ample time must be allowed.

(6) Austempering and Martempering. These are fairly advanced methods of heat treatment, much used in industry. Martempering is of little use to the model engineer, but Austempering *can* help, especially with the case we have just been discussing – the heat treatment of small springs. The process can best be understood by reference to a few diagrams. Fig. 43 shows the normal process of quenching and tempering, displayed on an "S" curve. The tempering period is not, of course, in any way connected with the time scale of the "S", because the transformations which occur are not the same as those within the "S". The diagram shows a high temperature temper, as might be used for a spring, and the material will end up as tempered Martensite; strong, tough, but not as hard as is needed for cutting tools.

In Fig. 44 the steel is quenched from a similar high temperature, but in a *hot salt bath*, somewhere between 280°C and 330°C, not cold water. The quenching temperature is higher than that at which the Martensite forms, and the transformation occurs along a line of constant temperature, as it passes through the two borders of the "S". After a time which depends on the period A-B, and the size of the work it is removed from the hot tempering bath and allowed to cool naturally in air. For silver steel the time for "spring temper" would be 16 minutes at around 320°C and 25 minutes at 300°C. The time increases markedly at lower temperatures – 45 minutes at 275°C and 2 hours at 250°C. No harm will be caused by slightly longer periods. The end result is not tempered Martensite, but a new structure (called Bainite, but don't let that worry you – it doesn't matter at all) which has very similar properties. The great advantage of this method is that there is no thermal shock during transformation to Martensite (or Bainite in this case) as there is with conventional quenching. Almost all commercially made springs – and such things as roll-pins and the like – are Austempered in this way.

The *Martempering* process is shown in Fig. 45, just for explanation, as its main use is when heat treating very thick or massive components. The piece is quenched from the high temperature in a

Fig. 44 *"Austempering" or constant temperature transformation. Thermal shock is eliminated and no tempering is needed.*

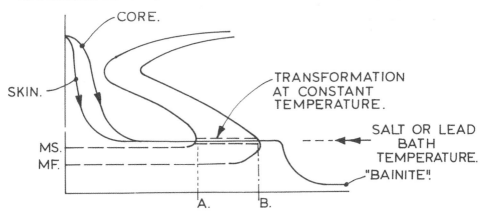

Other Heat Treatment Processes 79

salt bath as before, but instead of remaining there for transformation it is taken out as soon as it has reached the temper bath temperature and allowed to cool in air. It is subsequently tempered. The advantage over the conventional method is a reduction in the risk of distortion. There are no advantages to be gained for model engineers, as even the heaviest of our workpieces would be regarded as "tiddly bits" in industry, and would be Austempered.

The procedure (say as applied to springs) for *Austempering* to heat to a somewhat higher figure initially, say 900°C. The salt bath is prepared and brought up to the same temperature as would be needed for normal tempering – 300°C for a spring. As soon as the workpiece has been "soaked" for the necessary length of time it is *very quickly* – with the absolute minimum of delay- transferred to the hot salt bath. It is left there for a length of time which depends both on the type of steel and its thickness; 20 minutes will suffice for even the heaviest spring, and 30 minutes is all that would be needed of heat treating even a large crankpin in EN8. In this latter case, however, do remember that the maximum working temperature for a tempering salt bath is 500°C, and unfortunately you cannot quench the piece by setting it in a muffle furnace! However, most steels will give good heat treated conditions at this temper.

A few practical notes. First, this is a Heat Treating process, not a tool-hardening one. At Austempering temperatures below about 280°C the time required for the transformation increases very quickly, and might be as long as an hour at 250°C. For Austempering pieces requiring a higher temperature than can be achieved with the salt a lead bath may be used (lead melts at about 330°C). The high temperature salt bath can be used for initial heating if desired, and no harm will result from the carryover of this salt into the tempering bath. However, it is *most important* that no LOW temperature salt ever gets into the high temperature bath; as detailed in "Safety Precautions" a serious reaction can occur. Naturally, the hightemperature salt will solidify at the

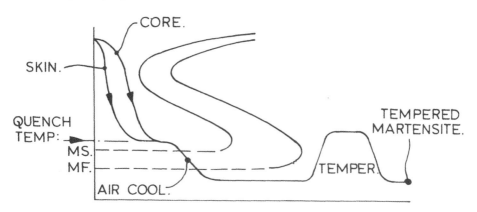

Fig. 45 *"Martempering"* This process is used for large or complex work where freedom from distortion is important. The work needs subsequent tempering.

tempering temperature and will collect in the bottom of the bath. This should be removed from time to time, but for the amount we use it is, perhaps, best to renew the tempering bath altogether when so much H.T.salt has set in the bath bottom as to interfere with heating.

As I remarked at the beginning, these are specialty processes, and do need a hot quenching bath. Model engineers have managed without them for almost 100 years, so that you need not worry about deciding to ignore them! However, if you HAVE got the equipment and the lead or salt, then it is worth a few experiments, especially if you make springs (leaf or coil) in any quantity. The process is ideal for small, complex parts made from medium carbon steel, which might distort if dealt with in the conventional manner.

(7) Cosmetic Heat Treatment. Not all heat treatment is done for strength, hardness, or other mechanical properties. It can be applied both to help resist corrosion, and – especially in instruments and – clocks for sheer decoration. In model work we may need to simulate the "as forged" condition, especially when the prototype is an early one.

Heat Blueing of steel (or "Browning" as the gunsmiths call it) is relatively easy – it is only necessary to heat the component to just over 300°C. However, the results will be less than satisfactory unless the preparatory work is well done. In the case where the part is to simulate "fine forgework" on the prototype it is a mistake to work for a polished finish. The surface should be fine matt, as produced by a *rotary* motion of sandpaper, the grade depending on the size of the part. The important point is to ensure that the surface, once prepared, is free from oil and grease and especially fingerprints. The latter will show up distressingly clearly after the heat treatment. Chemical degreasing should be followed by washing with hot detergent and water, and then air dried, after which it should be handled only with clean tissue paper; the "acid free" grade used by jewelers is best. A spirit lamp is best for small parts; larger may be heated in a sand bed or in one of the improvised muffles already referred to. Directly heating with a torch flame is unwise, as it is difficult to get even heating.

More decorative parts, as for screws in clocks and parts of instruments, or even clock hands, must be highly polished first, fine emery followed by polishing paper, until the finish is satisfactory. In this case there are differences of opinion; some hold that the final strokes of the polisher should be "in line" (or, for screwheads, done in the lathe) others hold that a random effect is more pleasing. You must try both and see which suits you best. It IS a matter of taste.

In all cases after heating to blue the parts are quenched in oil; not for any metallurgical reason, but because this provides an effective rust-proofing. The combination of the oxide layer and the oil seems to repel corrosive fumes. As to color, this has to be watched fairly carefully, as the "tints" of blue follow very closely. However, I find that for workshop tackle (which I "blue" for preservation rather than appearance) a shade of deep brown is not unpleasing, while many of my very early 19th century tools are straw colored. They are not carbon steel tempered, but look as if they have been so treated.

Blacksmith's Oxide is very difficult to simulate. This hard, corrosion resistant surface is the result (in full size) of some time at forging heat (1000°C) coupled with forge working. If a piece of mild steel is held at this temperature for any length of time some grain growth is inevitable. It doesn't

Other Heat Treatment Processes 81

matter if the piece *is* being forged, as this will correct matters, but it is difficult to do this with model parts. If it is practicable, the following procedure will give tolerable results. Arrange the manufacturing program so that any parts which matter (e.g., the journals and crankpins of a crankshaft) can be machined *after* the heat blacking is done. Bring the "forged" part to size and heat to bright red, giving a few light taps with a flat hammer to "distress" the surface. Dip in oil (don't quench right out) and again reheat, just for a few moments. Repeat the process, going up to bright red each time. Once satisfied with the "finish", normalize the steel as described on page 72 and then carry on with the machining, taking care not to damage the finish. Naturally if you can effect any actual forging, so much the better.

(8) Forging. It is, perhaps, apposite to deal with this now, having just remarked on the difficulty of forging model components! Most books on "Tempering & Hardening" published in the past lay great stress on the forging of lathe and shaper tools. This is very seldom done or needed – nowadays. Carbon steel tools are used only when High Speed tools are not available. Further, the *size* of tool we now use is much smaller than obtained even 50 years ago, when half-inch square shanks were common. Even a ⅜ in. square piece of stock will barely hold the heat long enough to give more than a couple of hammer blows, and with ⁵⁄₁₆ in., the more usual size these days, proper forging is almost impossible. However, there is the odd occasion when a tool must be slightly cranked, or a fly-cutter needs bending.

High carbon tool steel must be held to fairly close temperature limits while forging. At 0.7% carbon, as might be used for a special screwdriver, the maximum is 1050°C, and forging must stop when it falls to about 900°C. These temperatures can be used right up to about 1.0%.c. For 1.1% carbon and above, including silver steel, the temperature should be some 50°C lower, but the higher the carbon content the more care must be taken to avoid overheating. My experience is that with ⅜ in. square tools I can just get two blows in with the hammer before reheating is needed. I always give a full anneal before hardening after any but the very lightest forging operation. Ordinary mild steel can be forged much hotter – up to 1250°C according to some authorities – and is less subject to damage if forged cool, though I would prefer to normalize if much "black forging" has been done. In all cases overheating can ruin the metal, and carbon tool steel is especially at risk. There is *no* way in which a piece of overheated steel can be redeemed except by melting it down.

For detailed instructions in the use of blacksmiths' tools the reader is referred to one of the many books on "Wrought Ironwork" (though "iron" is seldom used these days) – it is a specialty craft in its own right. About the only use I make of forging tool steel is to reduce square section down to rectangular – less wasteful than machining it – and this does not call for anything more than keeping an eye on the temperature. Forging down the end of a pickaxe or crowbar (about 0.8% carbon) is easier, using a 5 lb. hammer, though my anvil, at 56 lb., is very light for such work.

(9) High Speed Steel. The hardening of high-speed tool-steel is really beyond the capacity of the majority of model engineers. To begin with, there are considerable variations in alloy content, ranging from 0.5% to 1.0% carbon, 0.5% to 4.0% Chromium, 0 to 18% Tungsten and some with 5% Cobalt – and they may

82 HARDENING, TEMPERING, AND HEAT TREATMENT FOR HOME MACHINISTS

include varying proportions of Molybdenum and Vanadium as well. Each demands its proper heat treatment and an approximation is not good enough – either the tool will crack or it will not be hard enough.

Second, the temperatures are high, with slow initial heating to the range 780-880°C followed by a fairly quick heating up to 1200 or 1300°C depending on the analysis. Most can then be cooled in air, but some require a partial oil-quench down to 500°C followed by air cooling. Tempering must follow immediately, and again there are wide variations in the requirements – in some cases tempering is done before the tool has cooled right down – from perhaps 150°C. The typical tempering temperature is about 550°C, but in some cases, especially for tools requiring considerable toughness (for roughing work on castings etc) a second tempering is carried out at (typically) 325°C.

The occasions when a high-speed tool requires rehardening are rare, and unless the exact analysis is known, and the workshop has precise temperature control of the furnace, this work is best left to the specialist. Even he will probably decline the work unless the source, type, and grade of metal is exactly known.

CHAPTER 8

The Measurement of Hardness

It is unlikely that many model engineers will be concerned with the actual measurement of hardness, but it is helpful to know HOW it is done when faced with one or other of the several "hardness numbers" used. The main difficulty is in deciding exactly what to measure, for "Hardness" is not easy to put on a scale. It is fair enough to say that steel which breaks under 50 ton/sq.in. is "twice as strong" as that which fails at 25 ton/sq.in., but we cannot be so definite with hardness numbers.

Mineralogists define hardness as "the ability to scratch" and use a scale called "Moh's scale" on which Diamond, the hardest, is No.10 and Talc ("French Chalk") is softest at No.1. On this scale Mild Steel would appear at No.6, and hardened tool-steel at No.7 – not a very big difference! A comparable test for metals uses a standard "scratcher" made of diamond carrying a definite load which is drawn across the surface of the metal. Load is adjusted to make a "standard width" of scratch, and this load is taken as a measure of the hardness. This test is now obsolete, but simple portable scratch test outfits are still used for casual "on site" hardness testing.

The majority of hardness testing done today depends on the *resistance to penetration* of the metal. In the Brinell test (Fig. 46) a hard steel ball, 10mm diameter, is impressed on the specimen of metal under a load of 3000 kilograms (about 3 tons). The diameter of the impression so formed is measured using a microscope with an internal scale. From this the surface area of the impression is calculated, and the surface stress obtained by dividing 3000kg by the area. The result is the "Brinell Number", which is, of course, a "stress" indicated in kilograms/sq.mm. This test is limited to about 500 Brinell number, as above this figure the ball itself distorts. For harder materials a tungsten carbide ball is used, while for soft materials the standard ball is used but the load is reduced – usually to 500 kg. – and a corresponding adjustment made to the formula. The Brinell numbers obtained agree within the standard limits.

The Rockwell hardness tester (Fig. 47) also uses a spherical impressor, but made from industrial diamond. However, the method and principle of operation are very different. The indenter, with a radius of 0.2mm, is first impressed into the specimen under a load of 10kg.

84 HARDENING, TEMPERING, AND HEAT TREATMENT FOR HOME MACHINISTS

Fig. 46 *A Brinell hardnes testing machine. (Courtesy Avery-Denison Ltd).*

This ensures that it is firmly seated in the specimen and that the specimen is secure on the supporting anvil. The dial indicating the depth of the impression is then zeroed. The "major" load, of 150kg for the most usual tests, is then applied at a steady rate controlled by a mechanism within the machine. After a set time – about 5 seconds – the major load is withdrawn. The dial then records the DEPTH of the impression caused by the major load and by this alone; there is no error due to "spring" in the machine frame or due to "settling down" of the specimen. Unlike the Brinell, the Rockwell hardness is a "number", not a surface stress, though the magnitude of this number can be correlated with such a stress.

The Rockwell machine can be used with several types of indenter and with several magnitudes of "major" load. For hard steel, and unhardened high carbon or alloy steels, the "Rockwell C" scale is used, but "Rockwell B", with a $\tfrac{1}{16}$ in. steel ball, is used for "mild" steels and some non-ferrous alloys. The "A" scale is used for extremely hard specimens and for thin, hard sheet material.

The advantage of the Rockwell test over the Brinell is that there is no need to measure the impression – the hardness can be read directly; it is, therefore, preferred for "Production" testing. Further, as the indenter can penetrate even hardened steel it can be used for materials beyond

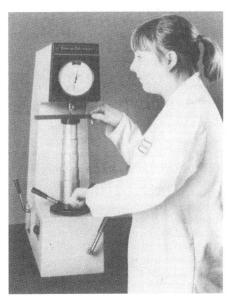

Fig. 47 *Hardness testing using a Rockwell type machine. The depth of the impression is shown on the large dial indicator. (Courtesy Avery-Denison Ltd).*

The Measurement of Hardness 85

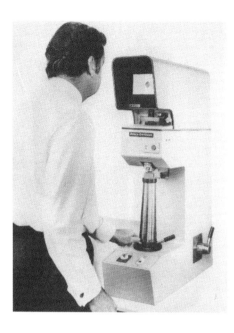

Fig. 48 *A Vickers type hardness tester. This machine has a projector microscope which throws an enlarged view of the impression on a screen. (Courtesy Avery-Denison Ltd).*

the range of the Brinell. The disadvantage is that it is not "Absolute" – it is, really, a hardness comparator and must be recalibrated from time to time.

Both the above make a visible impression in the material. The Vickers Diamond Pyramid (VDP) testing machine Fig. 48 uses a square based diamond pyramid as the indenter, with an included angle of 136°. The applied load is usually 50kg, but can be altered to suit special conditions (e.g., thin specimens or extra hard material). If this is done the magnitude of the load must be stated. The "across corners" dimensions of the impression are measured and tabulated values of "VDP Hardness" (in kg/sq.mm.) derived from the mean of the two. In the Vickers machine the microscope is "built in" and the specimen automatically registers for observation of the impression. The test is regarded as very accurate and, fortunately, the VDP numbers lie very close to the Brinell hardness number, so that "visualization" is easier than with the Rockwell scales. The main disadvantage of the Vickers machine is that the impression is very small, so that special surface preparation is required for really accurate work. The Rockwell machine requires only a "good machine finish". On the other hand, the Vickers does not disfigure the surface so much – the indentations are hardly noticeable. All three tests require the specimen to be brought to the machine. Hardness figures quoted in specifications and textbooks will all have been made on fairly robust specimens, to avoid any error due to specimen distortion under load, and all are subject to a small tolerance – generally a range of 1 or 2 digits on the Rockwell scale.

The Shore Scleroscope (Fig. 49) relies on a different principle. It is found that if specimens of reasonable size are used a ball-ended hammer will bounce to a degree which bears an almost linear relationship to the hardness. The Scleroscope is a portable hardness tester in which a small diamond-faced steel plunger is drawn up to a height of 10 inches within a glass tube. It is held there by a catch and, when released, falls on the specimen and rebounds up the tube. The amount of the rebound can be read from a scale. The succession of operations is automatically controlled by air-pressure generated from a rubber ball. This is a very useful instrument, and especially when tests must be made in the works – it is extensively used in steelworks for measuring the hardness of rolls in the mill. It leaves almost no impression at all, but care does have to be taken to avoid bouncing the hammer on the same place more than once, for the previous test will have work-hardened the surface.

The co-relation between Scleroscope numbers and VDP or Rockwell and Brinell is fairly good, *provided* the Scleroscope specimen was reasonably massive; the "standards" provided with the instrument are about one inch square × 2½ inch long. On very small pieces the specimen itself may bounce a little on the support anvil and this will cause a false reading. I have one of these (as seen in Fig. 49) picked up at an auction sale for a really silly price, and find that it gives excellent *comparative* figures when specimens are all the same size, but until the tool is over ½ in. square the results tend to be low when compared with tests done on the same piece with a Vickers instrument.

Comparison of Hardness Numbers. The choice of which test to use is often made from considerations other than "comparability". The Brinell machine is most often used for the softer grades of steel, and has the advantage that there is (for use on steel) a close relationship with the tensile strength; a Brinell test may often save the trouble of making a tensile test specimen. As already remarked the Rockwell test is quick, and much used in production workshops. The Vickers machine leaves very little evidence of its use, and because it is very accurate at high hardnesses it is naturally chosen for tool steels etc. Both the Vickers and the Brinell give the answer in kg/sq.mm. of impression, and agree closely at low hardness – below 220. With hard materials the fact that the Brinell ball may

distort and the Vickers diamond will not results in a divergence of the results. The "Shore" hardness readings are comparable with other tests only when the test specimen has a mass of at least one pound (0.5kg), but its indications are reliable when making comparisons – e.g., an increase from Shore 56 to 60 will imply a rise of approximately 100 points on the Vickers scale.

The table of comparisons given at the end of the book is drawn from a set prepared jointly by the American Society for Testing Materials, The American Metals Society, and the Society of Automotive Engineers, but British

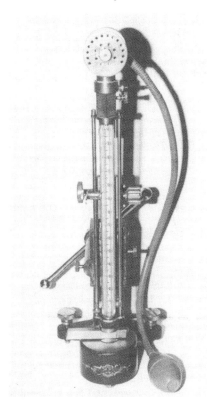

Fig. 49 *The author's Shore Scleroscope. This is a very early model, and differs in detail from those currently used.*

Standard No.860 – obtainable from most libraries – also gives comparative tables, and these go down to somewhat lower hardness. Great care must be taken in comparing the hardness of different classes of materials; the fact that, e.g., a steel and a heat treated aluminum alloy have the same hardness number will reflect the different characteristics of the two metals, and one may well be much harder than the other.

The hardnesses which may be expected from various classes of steel depend very much on the precision of temperature control, the effectiveness of the quench and, in some cases, the mass of the test specimen. The figures given in manufacturers' specifications are always obtained from standard test specimens, not working lathe tools. However, the following may give a guide to the "as quenched" state.

and tempered to 43 Rockwell could be machined at about 80 ft/min, and a Nickel-Chrome-Molybdenum alloy steel, hardened and tempered to about 48 Rockwell would need the speed reduced to around 55-60 ft/min for reasonable tool life.

The File Test. I have left this one till last! It is, of course, the "test of the first resort"; after quenching the piece is "shown to" a file, and if the latter slips off without cutting we know that it has hardened successfully. If, however, the file offers to cut the material, but doesn't quite manage it, then something has gone wrong; the hardness is not as high as it should be – for a high carbon steel, that is. Fine files will cut blue, or even purpletempered carbon steel, but should not make an impression on straw-colored tool points. If the workpiece *takes the edge off* the teeth of the file you have done very well indeed.

1.1-1.2C, 0.35Mn, 0.45Cr (Silver Steel)	66-67 Rockwell "C"
Chrome Manganese "non-shrink" die steel	64-65
Non-tempering chisel steel	52-54
22% Tungsten 12% cobalt high speed steel	65-66
18% Tungsten High speed steel	64-65
File Steel, 1.25% Carbon	68-69

The above figures will, of course, be considerably moderated by tempering; for carbon steel lathe tools, tempering to 150° will drop the hardness by no more than one point on the scale, and 200°C by twice as much. Carbon steel tempered to "blue" (310°C) is just machineable, at a Rockwell "C" figure in the region of 56-58. At the other end of the scale, freecutting mild steel, machineable at 200ft/min, will have a hardness equivalent to 11 on the "C" scale (which is not appropriate to metal as soft as this; the Brinell figure would be 180-185). A 1.8% Nickel 1.1% Chrome steel, oil quenched

Conclusion. The difficulty with hardness numbers is that though we know, subjectively, what hardness is, and what it does, it is very difficult to devise a means of measuring this quality. By convention, the surface stress needed to cause an indentation under a known load is used, but this clearly has limitations; a material which was very brittle would not accept an indenter without splintering. However, by custom the Brinell, Rockwell, and Vickers tests and, within its special application, the Shore, are accepted, and can be used for comparing different steels, or even different materials if due caution is used. The model engineer should not, however, be too concerned about an odd degree difference on the Rockwell or Brinell scales, or the equivalent on the Vickers, for it is very normal to find a difference of one point on Rockwell "C", or 30 divisions on the Vickers between different tests over the cutting surface of the same tool. These differences are partly due to "experimental error" in reading the microscope or dial, partly to differences in surface finish at the point of measurement, and partly to actual hardness differences. So, if you are offered a steel which hardens to 67, and the kind you normally use "only" gives 66, don't worry too much!

CHAPTER 9

Home Construction of Furnaces

Gas Firing. I have already referred briefly to the difficulties which arise with gas firing. The design of a combustion chamber does require specialty knowledge, and of a burner even more, *and* a lot of experiment. The ordinary "torch" – air or self-blown – is intended to produce a flame which can be directed *at* the work, whereas for heating a muffle you need one which distributes the heat sideways rather than vertically or "at a point". The "D"-shaped muffle referred to on page 57 is normally used on the Utile brazing hearth, which has a fixed sideburner as well as the two blow-torches. The firebricks supplied with the hearth are sized so that they can be arranged around the muffle itself to direct the flame properly. It is most effective, and when I was "on Town gas" I made considerable use of it. If you are considering a muffle of this kind, built into a homemade hearth, then a letter to William Allday & Co., Alcosa Works, Stourport on Severn, Worcs. DY13 9AP, should bring you details of the arrangement used, together with a quotation for the muffle.

A small "mufflette". I mentioned on page 58 and in Fig. 31 a small tube furnace which I rig up from time to time. Fig. 50 gives the details. The tube is a piece of 1½ in. bore steel exhaust pipe, about 16 gauge. For heating with a single propane burner it should not be more than 6 in. long, otherwise the heating will not be uniform. The end-supports are pieces of 1 in. thick Fossalcil bricks, with a hole bored through with a tank-cutter to suit the tube. You will notice that this hole is nearer the top of the brick than the bottom, to give space for the flame to develop properly below the tube. One of the cores from the holes is used as a permanent plug at the rear end and a homemade thermocouple (or even a commercial one) can be inserted through a hole in the center of it. The other core is slightly tapered and used to close the front end, holding it with tongs, of course.

The burner used is a Sievert No.2952, which is much too large, but can be throttled back once the tube is up to temperature. It is of the type which used to be known as a "Neck-tube" burner, with the air entrainment holes at the gasfeed end of the tube. Current types are known as "Cyclone" burners. The flame is directed to heat up the firebricks (or "Hotface" bricks) and NOT directed at the tube itself, which is heated by radiation from the hot brickwork.

90 HARDENING, TEMPERING, AND HEAT TREATMENT FOR HOME MACHINISTS

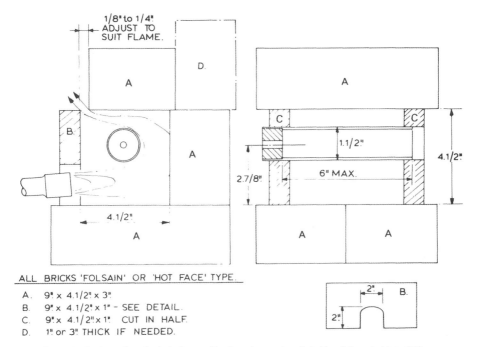

Fig. 50 Outline details of a small gas-fired tube furnace. The dimensions can be adjusted to suit the materials available.

In the photograph, Fig. 51, you can see that the burner is directed between two broken half-bricks on the left-hand side, but as a rule I use a full brick with a "mouse's hole" cut in the bottom. Hot gases escape from a gap between the top brick and this front one – a space of about ⅛ in. is sufficient. This little furnace heats up in about 5 minutes, and is not as expensive in gas as the burner size might suggest. Once the bricks are red hot the gas can be turned down considerably. There is no reason why such a furnace should not be made permanent, with the bricks cemented together with firecement, but I am a bit short of space in this department, so simply keep the two endplates and the tube and build up the rest when it

Fig. 51 The furnace in fig 50 in action.

Home Construction of Furnaces 91

is needed. I *have* used a 1-pint paraffin blowlamp in the same way, but this needed twice as long to get up to temperature. It would have been better, too, had all the bricks been of the Fossalcil type. But it did the work required at around 780°C.

Naturally, a smaller diameter tube can be used, but if it is at all longer than the 6 in. (about 4½ in. "hot length") you may need two smaller burners, or keep moving the larger one from side to side. I have been meaning for a long time to devise a fan-shaped head for the burner, like those used on paint-stripping torches, but have not had the time! Such a head would distribute the heat sideways much better. Furnace control would be easier, too. In this connection, you must not be tempted to hurry things up by heating the tube directly, for it will only grow cold again. Once the firebrick is hot it is only a case of minor adjustments to the burner to keep a steady temperature, and once the bricks are hot all over the muffle tube keeps pretty steady.

Electric Heating. This is much easier for the home constructor, but the furnace will be markedly slower in reaching the operating temperature. You will appreciate that a burner such as that just mentioned has a maximum output of something like 18 kW, and an electric element of that capacity would strain your power supplies somewhat! On the other hand, electric heating is clean, silent, and easy to control – automatically if need be. There is little risk from fire. The one thing that must be borne in mind, however, is that you are dealing with lethal voltages and must pay really strict attention to safety rules as well as to the I.E.E. regulations. All metal parts must be earthed, suitable insulation materials applied and – rule No. 1 – the supply should ALWAYS be switched off when charging

or discharging the work. The material from which wirewound muffles or heating tubes are made is not a perfect insulator. **Wound Muffles.** Furnace muffles ready wound are available from Messrs Gallenkamps, Griffin & George Ltd, and other laboratory equipment suppliers. They are, in fact "spares" for furnaces similar to that seen in Fig. 32. Special insulating material will be needed adjacent to the muffle itself, and this, too, can be had from the same source. Outer insulation can be the glass- or slag-wool insulation used in (e.g.) AGA cookers around the firebox. A minimum of 3 in. of *good* heat insulation is required, otherwise the heat loss to the case will prevent the furnace from reaching its proper temperature – the element rating is only about 2 KW. The outer case itself is – or was – usually Syndanyo sheet, about ½ in. thick, joined with self-tapping screws, but as this contains asbestos it is now replaced by similar material based on Calcium Silicate. This *may* be available from hardware stores but if in difficulty Messrs Cape Insulation Ltd, Washington, Tyne & Wear NE38 8JL, (or at their local offices) can give the address of the nearest retailer.

The actual arrangement of the furnaces is a matter for your own taste and ingenuity! Don't forget that the door needs insulating (a piece of hot-face brick will serve) and, if it has a metal handle, this needs earthing. You can add a pyrometer – indeed, I would most strongly advise this, as the virtues of muffle heating are considerably diminished otherwise. These can, of course, be obtained from the same source as the muffle, complete with flange for screwing to the case and a bracket to hold the indicator. Commercial furnaces are equipped with a "thermal fuse"; this is no more than a pair of rods projecting into the chamber, insulated of course, united with a wire of

Fig. 52 *The Kanthal electric furnace built from a kit. (Courtesy Kanthal Electroheat Ltd).*

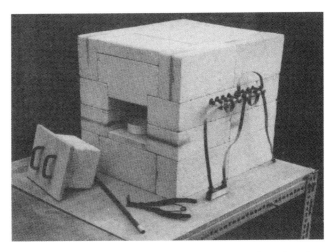

suitable melting point (silver for 1000°C, for example) and wired in series with the winding. If the furnace over-runs and gets too hot the fuse melts and cuts off the supply.

A Radiant Element Furnace Kit. Fig. 52 is a photo of a furnace designed by Kanthal Electroheat Ltd, Inveralmond, Perth PH1 3EE specifically for home construction. (The photo was taken, by the way, before the essential earthed guard had been equipped over the terminals). It can be built either as an 8 KW unit rated at 1350°C or with a 4 KW loading for 1200°C. The latter is probably adequate for all model engineering purposes. The heating elements in this case are Silicon Carbide rods, the ends of which can be seen in the photo, and these are set in the top of the chamber. Heating is entirely radiant, but I would advise users to bring the furnace up to temperature before putting in any work, otherwise the upper surface is liable to be heated faster than the lower. The furnace body is made entirely of Hot Face Insulating Bricks which are sawn and drilled to the detail drawing supplied by Kanthal, but the chamber base is a special refractory plate which will stand more wear and tear than will the surface of the bricks. Fig. 53 shows sectional views of the furnace – the size is, of course, determined by the number of elements used. Thermostat control is available, but very expensive, and a simple energy controller is really very adequate. A thermocouple/pyrometer is an essential if the best is to be got out of the equipment. This, once built up, is a professional furnace without the normal casing and hinged or sliding door, and the chamber size is more than adequate for most model engineers.

Electric Tube Furnace. Over the years a number of homemade electric tube furnaces have been described, using ordinary electric fire elements and home fired ceramic tubes. There are several hidden problems. The first is that such elements are rated to work in free air – i.e. losing heat as fast as they can. Once they are encased in insulating material they will rapidly burn out. They must be derated for furnace work. Second, it is not easy to make a fire-cement tube without

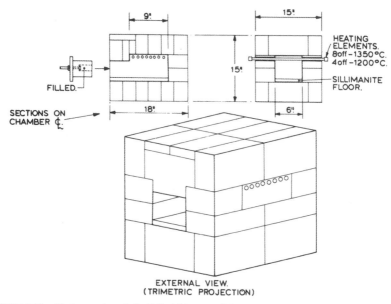

Fig. 53 *Outline details of the furnace shown in Fig 52:The bricks can easily be cut without special tools.*

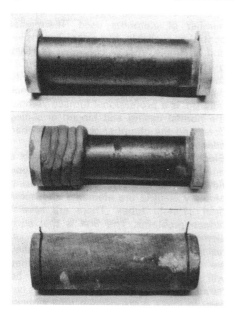

blisters and spalling. Third, such a tube is usually very fragile, and it cannot be strengthened by molding it around a steel tube as some makers have suggested; the expansion of the tube will burst the clay.

However, for those willing to experiment, and face one or two failures with equanimity, Fig. 54 shows the stages in making the tube. The "mold" is a piece of steel tube of the desired internal diameter, furnished with two thickness washers. Waxed paper is wound around the tube – three layers – and the endplates or spacers are greased. The firecement (that seen is "Kos") is made into "worms" of thickness just over half the desired thickness of the tube. (This

Fig. 54 *The tube former, which should be covered with waxed paper, winding a "worm" (the paper is not shown in the photo) and the tube after firing. The wire binding acts as an anchor for the element at each end.*

94 HARDENING, TEMPERING, AND HEAT TREATMENT FOR HOME MACHINISTS

Fig. 55 *Winding the element in the lathe. Note the notch in the wooden guide.*

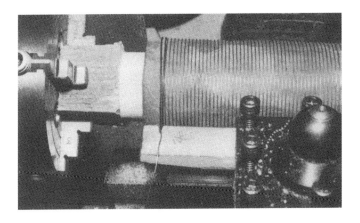

should not be more than ¼ in. and ³⁄₁₆ is better). These worms are then wound around over the paper liner and well kneaded together. The first layer is allowed to air dry, and then a second laid on top, this one being smoothed and kneaded down using the two end washers as guides. This too, is air-dried for several days on a hot radiator, after which the tube is withdrawn. If it sticks, a blowlamp can be directed down the inside to fire the paper, but on no account must the firecement tube be made really hot at this stage. With the steel tube extracted the cement must be further air-dried, and the longer this lasts the better – up to a week. It must then be "fired", and this process must also be very slow. (The problem is that moisture in the interior may form steam pockets which lift the surface). Fire from the inside with a brazing torch, *very* slowly raising the temperature to red heat. If any spalls form, these can be picked off and "patched" with firecement.

You will need two elements, from the local electric store, of 1 KW rating. Carefully unwind one by threading a length of ³⁄₁₆ in. rod through and pulling off the wire. Avoid kinks. Measure the length, and then wind on to a bobbin. Unwind part of the second element, and cut off one fifth of its length. Double this and twist, to make a twin wire. This will then be cut in two to form the connecting wires, and also serves to reduce the applied voltage to the actual heating element. You will need two small connectors made by drilling ¼ in. steel rod ⅛ in. and tapping for two small set-screws; the

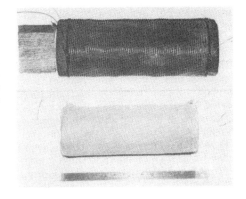

Fig. 56 *The wound element, with one of the wooden plugs at the left-hand end, and the element after coating with cement to retain the coils – before firing.*

Home Construction of Furnaces 95

Fig. 57 *A pot furnace suitable for temperatures up to 950°C.*

standard brass connectors will not do, as the temperature is too high.

Make two wooden plugs to fit inside the cement tube, one with a center hole in it. Wind iron wire around each end of the tube, about ⅜ in. from the end, and twist tightly; these are the anchor points for the ends of the element. This will be wound on using the lathe.

From the known length of the element and the diameter of the tube you can calculate the number of turns. Select an easy screw-cutting pitch which will permit this number of turns on the bobbin – something between 12 and 14 tpi will probably serve. Set a piece of wood in the toolholder with a notch to guide the wire (Fig. 55) and attach one end of the element to the tailstock end anchor, leaving about three inches free. Keep a fair tension on the wire and with the lathe running at about 50 rpm, wind on the wire. At the other end, anchor the wire again. Note; if you have more than a foot left over but less than a yard, don't worry, but if there is more than that you should re-wind with a finer pitch. If the winding does not reach the end, use your judgment as to whether to tolerate a short unheated part of the tube or to coarsen the pitch. This part of the job takes very little time. Fig. 56 shows the wound tube.

The winding must now be covered with a very thin layer of cement – the wire should just show. This, once set, will form a binding to prevent adjacent coils touching when the wire expands with heat. Before going any further, test the arrangement. Attach the two twin feeder/voltage dropper lengths, one at each end, and a piece of house cable to these with the normal twin porcelain jointer, Make sure that there is no risk of any part of the bare wire touching anything, and set all on a piece of firebrick. Use a plug with 13 amp fuse and switch on. DON'T TOUCH ANYTHING. After a short while the tube should start to get hot, and you must note the final temperature. If this is no better than black, pull out the plug, cut about one fifth off each of the twisted end lengths and try again. If it gets to dull red and stays there, all should be well; once insulated it should reach the desired temperatures. If, however, it burns out after half an hour, you need more on the twisted end lengths!

Once satisfied it is worth doing the rest of the work. Insulate the feeder wires with ceramic beads, and then make up a casing of insulating bricks carved out, feeding the wires outward between two bricks. Make a terminal block from ¼ in. Syndanyo and attach this to one of the bricks. (If you use bolts, then these must be earthed, as must the protective cover over the terminals if of metal). How you arrange this is up to you, but you need *at least* three inches of insu-

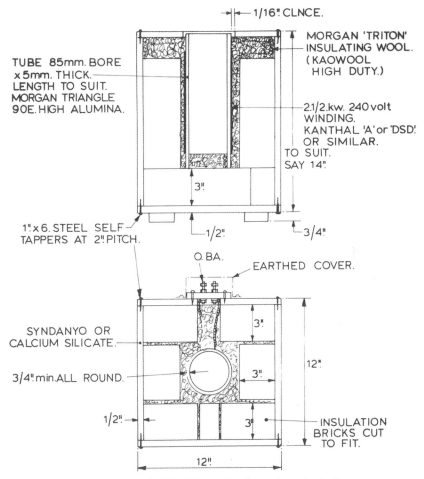

Fig. 58 *Outline details of a furnace similar to Fig 57. Detail changes have been made to reduce heat losses.*

lating brick all around. Any gaps can be filled with ground-up fragments. Close the back of the tube with a brick plug, and (for what it is worth) just lean a firebrick against the other end to act as a "door".

I give these instructions "without warranty"! I have made such a furnace and had satisfactory results, but have also had three burn out on me after some months of service, and several give way at once. Others have built them and had them in service for years. A great deal depends on (a) the homogeneity of the cement; it must be well kneaded before and during application, and (b) the quality of the element. You can, of course, buy the suitable resistance wire from Kanthal, specified for this service, and this will not

Fig. 59 Welded steel pot. Note the earth terminal.

need derating and be less likely to "blow" at the operating temperature. (The wire may get up to 1200°C with the tube at 900°C). You can, of course, buy a tube, too, from Morgan Refractories Ltd; but if you are going to do that you might as well buy a ready-wound tube, either from Kanthal Electroheat or from Morgans and have done with it!

High Temperature Salt Furnace. Fig. 57 shows my 2¾ in. × 10 in. neutral salt furnace for temperatures up to about 950°C, rated at just under 2.8 KW. This is, perhaps, much larger than might be needed, and a 2½ in. × 8 in. would do for most applications, but it was originally made (not by me) as a small laboratory furnace. Fig. 58 is the drawing. The tube is 3⅜ in. bore Morgan 90E High Alumina wound with a Kanthal element for 240 volts. If buying a wound tube it is important to specify the power input – 2½ to 2¾ KW in this case – the applied voltage, and the operating temperature of the ceramic tube. This will be higher than that in the salt pot itself, so that a sketch of the arrangement, or a copy of Fig. 58, should be sent with the inquiry. The outer casing is of ½ in. Syndanyo, though today one of the Calcium Silicate substitutes from Cape Insulation Ltd would be used. The immediate insulation material around the element is "Triton" Kaowool ceramic fiber, supplied by Morgan Ceramic Fibres Ltd, Bromborough, Wirral L62 3PH. The standard grade is good for 1250°C, but I suggest the "High Duty" rated at 1400°C. This is packaged into the space between the element itself and the heat insulating bricks – which are cut roughly to leave about 1 inch gap between their surface and that of the element. The bottom of the tube is packed with the wool also, but this must not lie above the first coil of the element.

Fig. 59 shows the actual pot. This is made from drawn steel tube, with the bottom welded on with full thickness penetration. The O.D. of the pot must be about ⅛ in. less than the bore of the heater tube, so that it may be necessary to machine the steel tube to a smaller thickness. This is not difficult and a rough finish will do. The support flange is recessed as shown. This prevents any splashes of salt from getting between the pot and the heater. The handle shown is not intended for carrying the pot around when hot, but simply to make it easier to lift. A lid of some kind is needed, both to

Fig. 60 *The furnace of Fig. 57 with the lid removed. That in Fig. 58 has more and different insulation.*

keep out dirt when not in use, and to cover the pot when reheating. There is just a slight risk that the lower layers of salt may melt and expand before the crust on top melts, and if the latter splits open under the pressure there could be a spitting out of hot liquid. Fig. 60 shows the furnace with the top cover removed. This furnace has less insulation than is desirable.

None of the dimensions is critical – you can make the size of the heater tube or melting pot to suit your needs and adjust all to suit. However, it *is* important to allow for plenty of insulation – the more the better as this will speed up melting time and reduce current consumption once up to temperature. Reducing the diameter of the pot will not reduce the overall size of the case very much. As to depth, you have to allow sufficient for the tide to rise as you immerse the workpiece, and the top level of molten salt must always be below the top of the winding. The loading of the heating element depends almost directly on the volume of the pot, but I don't advise going below 1000 watts (1 KW) as the heat losses are by no means negligible.

Note that the steel pot and the terminal box (if of metal) MUST both be earthed, as the insulation resistance of the ceramic tube is not perfect. (The current should, of course, be switched off when manipulating the work). There is no real need to insulate the leads to and from the heating element, but the little ceramic beads used on cooker circuits and electric fires are very adequate. The actual leads are a continuation of the heater winding, but doubled and twisted, so that they will not get very hot. The terminal block is of Syndanyo or Calcium Silicate, though porcelain terminal blocks are sometimes available on the "surplus" market. The regulation of the furnace is best done with an "Energy Controller" – a thermostatic control would be very expensive. Those on electric cookers will handle 3 KW. I do not advise building it into the furnace casing, as these controllers incorporate a thermal switch to effect the time-intervals, and the heat from the furnace would upset them.

"Heater Bricks". A relatively new development is in the form of a heat insulating brick with a heater element embedded in the face. At first sight these would seem to be the ideal module for the construction of a small furnace. There is also a variation, with the "brick" in the form of a hollow tube, making the basis of a tube furnace. There are two problems – the first is that the units are wound for no more than 60 volts, so that either a hefty transformer is needed, or one must use four units. The second is that the hot face of the bricks will not carry any load; you would need a supporting and "heat transparent" floor, or a metal tube if using the tubular type. Both floor and tube would have to be of heat resisting steel or of considerable thickness if any reasonable life was to be expected. However, these are not difficult problems to get over and readers who are interested in this development should write to Messrs W.J. Furse & Co., Ltd, Wilford Road, Nottingham NG2 1EB. The bricks are known as "Watlow Ceramic Fiber Heaters".

Resistance Wire. This is obtainable from the Kanthal firm already referred to, from London Electric Wire & Smiths Co. (LEWCOS) Church Road, London E10, as well as other manufacturers, and in small quantities from K.R. Whiston, New Mills, Stockport Cheshire. Such element wire is available either as the normal round wire or as strip, the latter for the higher KW ratings. The material must be selected for the operating temperature *of the wire,* which will be higher than that of the work by quite a bit, and this does mean that the advice of the manufacturers, with their vast experience, is needed. To "play safe" and select the highest rated element wire can be expensive.

The problem is to effect a compromise between three variables. The overall

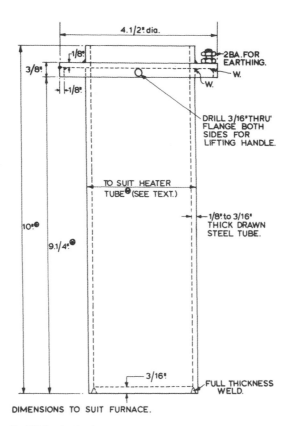

Fig. 59A *Construction details of the pot shown in Fig. 59.*

resistance needed to limit the current to the desired power – e.g., for 1 KW at 240V the resistance at the working temperature must be such as to limit the current to 1000/240 = 4.17 amp, say 58 ohms. Next, the surface area of the wire must be such that it can dissipate this power. A not untypical rating is 6.5 watts/sq. inch of surface area. So long as the length of wire needed for this criterion is *less* than that needed to provide the required ohmic resistance the element will be safe, but if the opposite condition holds, then it will probably burn out. Finally, there must be enough room to wind this calculated length of wire on the ceramic tube. It is not safe to wind at closer pitch than about 14 T.P.I., as there is then risk of adjacent turns touching each other.

The following calculation table shows how four gauges of wire have been assessed to meet the required criteria for a 1 KW 240 volt heater element. Note that these figures, though typical, should not be used in an actual furnace; the table is just an exercise to show how to go about the job.

Required current = 1000/240 = 4.17 amp. Required resistance at the operating temperature of 1200°C, 240/4.17 = 57.6 ohm. Power capacity of the wire 6.67 watts/sq.in. surface area, hence A = 150 sq.ins. Outside diameter of heater tube is 4 in. = 1.05 ft circumference.

power output if wound to a resistance of 57.6 ohm. The 19 gauge element will need a winding length of about 7 inch, and this is reasonable for 4 inches diameter – or it could be wound at 12 TPI over an 8-inch length if desired.

The resistance per foot and surface area per foot (or in metric units) is quoted by the suppliers, as is the safe dissipation in watts per unit area of wire. In some cases it may be necessary to change to flat strip heaters, in order to match the resistance per foot to the required surface area. The wire manufacturers will be able to supply tables which help considerably, but do not expect them to act as "Consultants" for the price of a few pounds worth of wire. (The 19 gauge element tabled would need about £9 worth).

Conclusion. This chapter has necessarily been brief, for furnace-making is not a very common occupation for model engineers, and there is not much published information. However, I hope that what I have written will help you to avoid some of the more difficult problems. I would, however, suggest that before embarking on the manufacture of any but the simplest muffle you explore the second-hand market. Facebook Marketplace may bring forth something, and even if the furnace requires a new muffle, or perhaps the thermocouple of the pyrometer, the cost of repair may well

Wire Gauge	Length Reqd, Ft.		Turns on 4 in. dia	Winding Length inches.
	For Power	For Resistance		
16	62.2	259	246	17
18	82.9	146	139	10
19	99.3	104	95	6.8
20	110.3	82.4	78	5.6

This table shows that the 20 gauge wire requires a greater length to dissipate the power than is needed to offer the required resistance; it is, therefore, unsuitable. All the others will handle the

be less than the cost of materials for a homemade affair. The little gas-fired tube furnace is, of course, a very simple matter, as you must have firebricks around any heat-treatment hearth anyway.

CHAPTER 10

Safety Precautions

Safety in the workshop is, most of the time, no more than "applied common sense", and I fear that many of the Parliamentary Enactments on the subject seem to assume that most people working in industry are half-wits. However, common sense is the more easily applied if something is known of the hazards, and my object in this chapter is to present these to you, no more. To those readers who have been given this advice all their lives I can only say that many others have not; and if YOU tried to use *their* tools you might well do yourself an injury straight away.

Fire. This is, perhaps, the most obvious danger. At 780°C the workpiece will, if left, burn a hole in the floor – or through your boot. Worse, it can burn through your gas-hose in seconds, and though the hose failure valve (dare I assume that your equipment has one?) will shut off the supply, the initial burst of flame can set fire to other things. The second hazard is from the heating flame itself. The practice of moving the torch aside to observe the metal is normal, but how many practitioners think on as to where the flame is now pointing? I have myself set fire to a carelessly placed piece of cotton waste this way.

The answer to these is twofold. First, the heat-treatment spot should be as fireproof as possible. If working on a bench, then the top should be covered with two layers of bricks, with staggered joints, so that flame cannot pass through. Better, use a specially built steel frame with the bricks set in. I know that space often compels the use of wooden top bench, but if any great amount of heat treatment is done then the bench should be made accordingly. The brazing spot should be so equipped, and this is, surely, the right place to do other "hot work" as well.

Second, have fire-extinguishing gear available. Fire can get out of hand very quickly indeed, and prompt action may save you a lot of misery – and money. The quench bucket is the first resource, of course (but note later the remarks on salt baths) sand is the second, and a proper fire extinguisher the third. I use the "Dry Powder" type, and have a CO_2 extinguisher as a back-up. (We are 12 miles from the fire station). These types are both safe for use on electrical fires, and my workshop, like yours, has a lot of wiring in it. A very sensible arrangement is for the whole of the bench (brazing or heat treatment) to stand in a shallow tray con-

102 HARDENING, TEMPERING, AND HEAT TREATMENT FOR HOME MACHINISTS

taining an inch or so of DRY sand. This will catch any droppings safely, and from it a quick shovelful of sand can contain a small fire while reaching for the extinguisher.

The other hazard from hot metal is burning *yourself.* The first point to note is that cold water won't hurt a burn, and to put any kind of dressing over a dirty paw is asking for trouble. So, sluice on cold water and get someone carefully to wash the area around the burn. Then if it is a bad one – red-hot metal on the back of the hand, for example – or of any size, do NOT apply anything sticky. A dry burn dressing will do little harm, but even a clean pad made from a clean handkerchief (NOT lint) and loose bandage will keep the lesion clean on the way to "Casualty" at the local hospital. Don't neglect this – a burn attended to promptly by experts will give little trouble, but leave it till next day and you may well be in trouble. For minor burns, then the acriflavene based burn dressings can be used, but even here, seek the advice of your doctor if in doubt. Keep these dressings in the workshop or nearby, but don't forget – it is the dirt around the burn which will cause infection, so see that your paws are clean.

Clothing. What is up must come down, and your feet are vulnerable. Carpet slippers are not the best things to wear with metal at 800°C a couple of feet higher up. Wear leather shoes. Cotton twill overalls are safe – or as safe as can be – but those of man-made fiber can literally melt if overheated. Splashes from quench-tanks can be hot, and those from salt baths ARE hot. Protect your throat and neck. On the steelworks we used to have sweat rags which could be held in our teeth. (Though nowadays I have no doubt that special hot-metal clothing is de rigueur!). But an old scarf is useful – nothing is worse than a hot piece of scale jumping off a tool in the quench and lodging down the open neck of a shirt! The use of gloves is debatable. If these tend to make you clumsy and increase the risk of dropping workpieces then perhaps better to do without them. But if you have a pair of reasonably supple *chrome leather* ones, these should be worn when working with hot high-temperature salt (or molten lead if you use that). There are some so-called "heat proof" gloves on the market, but they are not suitable for this class of work – maybe at tempering temperatures, but they won't stand red-hot metal. The object of the glove is, of course, to protect your hand from accident, not to enable you to pick up workpieces! One important point – the gloves should be such that you can whip them off quickly; they will keep the heat from the hot metal from your paw, but the glove is then hot, and this heat will travel through soon afterward. Finally, wear a cap. Quench a piece of steel with a hole in it, and the odds are that a lump of superheated water will leap up, to land on your bald patch. (So you have hair? Good, but it would go through that, too!). There is absolutely no need to dress up as if you were melting 100 tons of steel when you are about to harden a ⅜ in. form tool, but that tool IS hot, and you should, as I said at the beginning, use your common sense.

Splashes. You may well have dumped a few jobs into the pickle-bath in the past, so you know what happens. Don't lean over the quench tank, and if the work is of any size at all, wear suitable goggles. These are dirt cheap, but MUST be to British Standard 2092/2 or OSHA (ANSI) Z87.1-2010. These are heat-proof and will not shatter from heat as glass will. They have little side-pieces that stop things from coming that way, and can be worn over glasses. They also have a little "top shelf" which prevents stuff from falling into the space between specs and the eyes. If you do get anything in your eye, wash well with cool water and go to the doctor; it is just not worth taking any risk here.

Splashes from the oil-quench tank need be no more serious than from water – they should not be too hot – but if at all painful treat as for a burn; wash around the spot and apply a dry burn dressing until you can get medical attention. The brine bath differs only from the water quench in that the salt is an irritant. But don't neglect any injury from hot splashes, from water, brine, or oil. The point is not so much that they are hot as that they are DIRTY, and it is from this that subsequent infection can arise.

Salt Baths: General. ALL hot liquid baths are dangerous if they can over-turn. The first rule, therefore, is that the furnace, or if used, the hotplate for tempering salt, should be secure in this respect. A heavy pot on top of a flimsy stove is just *not* acceptable and if you are unable to arrange for really solid support, don't use the system at all. Second, the salts – sodium nitrite and potassium nitrate for tempering, and sodium and potassium chloride for Austenising, are, though strictly non-toxic, irritating; just like kitchen salt. The cold salt should not be handled with bare hands, and any powder spilled should be dealt with using a brush and shovel.

All salts can absorb a little water, and all contain "water of crystallisation" until melted. At first melt, therefore, there will be quite a bit of frothing as this water is expelled. Start the melt with the pot only half-full, and apply heat very slowly. Let the initial froth die down – don't increase the temperature – and then add a little more salt. Use a metal scoop to put it in; don't "pour it out of the bag". Let the moisture evaporate and again add more salt, in small quantities at a time, until the required amount is in the pot. Allow plenty of space for the tide to rise when work is put in. In the case of the electrically heated high-temperature furnace the salt level should be below the upper end of the element.

There will be no frothing on remelting so long as you have had a lid on so that it cannot absorb any moisture, and even then it will be relatively slight. However, it is worth again repeating that the salt may form a crust, and when re-melted the expansion of the liquid below may cause this to crack and send out a spurt of hot salt. So, keep a substantial lid on the pot until the whole is melted.

Never stick your head over the top of a salt pot in service, always observe at an angle, always wear BS2092 grade 2 "Impact" goggles and a cap. and gloves if you can possibly manage with them.

All work put into the bath must be water- and oil-free, and should be immersed slowly. Particular care must be taken when oil-quenched work is to be tempered at above about 220°C, as any residual oil may "flash off". Prior degreasing is recommended if the tempering bath is above 245°C. Slight surface oil contamination should cause no trouble in the Austenising bath, but if there are any holes in the workpiece these should be cleared of oil before immersion. No fixtures or other devices for use in salt baths should be made from tube. Great care should be taken to ensure that no foreign matter falls into the bath, whether cold or hot. It is imperative that no water should fall into a salt bath, and water should not be used to extinguish any fire adjacent to one.

Avoid overheating any salt bath. They should not be left "on heat" when leaving the workshop for more than the odd minute or two, even if thermostatic control is equipped. Overheating can be

104 HARDENING, TEMPERING, AND HEAT TREATMENT FOR HOME MACHINISTS

serious with tempering salt if temperatures go above about 550°C. ON NO ACCOUNT MUST TEMPERING SALT GET INTO THE AUSTENISING POT. **Tempering Salt.** This is a mixture of Sodium Nitrite and Potassium Nitrate. These can irritate the skin, but are classed as "non toxic". Soap and water can be used to wash off the skin, and an eyewash solution if any powder gets in the eyes. The salt looks like colored sugar, so that it SHOULD BE KEPT AWAY FROM CHILDREN, but if any is taken by mouth give plenty of water to drink and call the doctor. In the event of a burn from molten salt – (a) Flood the affected area with water or Sodium Bicarbonate solution (b) Remove solidified salt and wash again (c) treat as a thermal burn; apply a medicated (dry) burn dressing and see the doctor or, if extensive, take the patient to the hospital.

The salt is not inflammable in itself, but a strong supporter of combustion; wood or cloth contaminated with the salt will burn vigorously. Some organic compounds can react vigorously with the salt when heated. Care should be taken that splashes or spillages of powder on wood or rubber are cleaned up promptly. Clothing should be washed, NOT dry-cleaned, as there is a reaction with dry-cleaning solutions.

If heated above 550°C, oxides of nitrogen may form, and these can be absorbed by the skin, and if inhaled can be dangerous. Symptoms are blueness of the lips and face, and perhaps shortness of breath. The condition requires medical treatment.

The salt is supplied in plastic bags, and should be ladled from these into the pot with a metal spoon or ladle. Storage containers should be moisture-proof; I keep mine in plastic bags inside large Nescafe cans. Used salt can be disposed of by washing down the sink with a good flood of water.

Within the temperature range and quantities used by model engineers this salt can be regarded as non-hazardous provided reasonable care is taken. **High-temperature (Austenising) Salt.** This is a mixture of Sodium Chloride (common salt) and Potassium Chloride. It is virtually non-harmful and can be treated as if it were household salt if it gets in the eyes, in a cut, or is taken by mouth. In the event of burns from molten salt these should be treated as for the tempering salt, but the burn may be severe and immediate resort to the casualty department of the hospital is recommended.

Spillage of the cold salt powder is unimportant, though it will absorb water and may damage (rust) metal. Spillage of hot salt can be contained with dry sand dams, and the fire, if any, tackled with CO_2 extinguishers; water should not be used in the presence of molten salt.

Material immersed in the bath *must* be dry, and the work should be set in slowly to allow any air trapped in holes to escape slowly – a rapid immersion may cause spurting. Care must be taken when remelting, with a substantial lid, in case a crust forms on the top of the bath, and initial melting must be slow; this salt melts at about 670°C, so that frothing at this stage should be reduced to a minimum with the depth of the bath being increased only slowly.

This salt is inherently safe, but the hazard from very hot liquid is present. If treated as a molten metal, with the same precautions, dangerous situations are unlikely to arise, (though I repeat my previous warning; on no account allow any tempering salt, or metal contaminated therewith, to get into the high-temperature salt, cold or hot.) Careful attention to protective clothing at all times

Safety Precautions 105

is the order of the day. Storage and disposal conditions are the same as for Tempering salt.

Electrical. Electrical hazards in the heat-treatment shop are exactly the same as those elsewhere, but more care must be taken over trailing leads. Metal at quenching temperature will burn through insulation and cause a short-circuit very quickly, and will itself set the insulation on fire. Wires within furnace casings should be insulated with ceramic beads, obtainable from the local Electricity Service depots. Glass-fiber insulating sleeving is available, but this is normally rated only for the temperatures found in domestic cookers. ALL metal parts of a furnace must be properly earthed, the earth wire being not less in diameter than the main leads and preferably more. These connections, especially when earthing a hot point (e.g. the pot in a salt furnace) must be inspected and cleaned reguarly, as oxide formation may set up an unacceptable earth leakage resistance.

Cables to the supply socket must be routed away from risk of contact with flame, hot metal, or salt and, if permanent, covered by metal shield or conduit – which must be earthed. Fusing is best done at the 3-pin plug-top, but if fused elsewhere (or if circuit breakers are equipped to the control box) these must be arranged to break the "Line" circuit only; on NO account must any fuse be set in the "Neutral" conductor. Failure of a fuse here leaves the apparatus live to earth.

Finally, because no furnace muffle is a perfect insulator, it is common prudence to switch off the circuit when handling the work. This applies especially to muffle furnaces; a salt pot with an earthed pot should be very safe so long as the earth connection is sound.

Conclusion. The careful practitioner will meet few dangers in heat treatment, but no amount of "precautions" will save the careless from injury. Heat treatment practice is probably less dangerous than brazing, as though temperatures may be higher the amount of heat present is less. If, in this chapter, I have been "teaching my betters how to suck eggs" I console myself with the thought that a hot egg is hard-boiled, and such cannot be blown at all. Any material much above 70°C needs to be treated with respect!

APPENDIX 1

Thermocouples and Pyrometers

It is possible to obtain mercury-in-glass thermometers which will safely register up to 360°C very cheaply, and nitrogen filled mercury thermometers in special glass can be had which read to 600°C. They are very fragile, but can be used for tempering – though I make a steel protecting sheath for mine. The well-known "Rototherm" temperature indicators, based on a bi-metallic coil, can be bought to read up to 300°C (they are used as oven thermometers) and are more robust. The mercury-in-steel dial thermometers will operate safely up to 650°C, but they are both expensive and bulky. None of these, however, will serve for temperature indication when heating (Austenising) for quench hardening. The thermo-electric pyrometer is the only practicable answer.

Fig. 61 shows the principle. If the junction between the two wires at "A" is heated, and that at "B" is kept cool, then the meter "M" will show that a voltage is developed which depends on the temperature difference at the two junctions. Note that it is the temperature DIFFERENCE which matters; if the meter shows a voltage corresponding to 700°C, and "B" is at 80, then the temperature at "A" will be about 780°C.

Further, the EMF generated does not vary exactly with the temperature; plotting EMF against temperature difference shows a slight curve to the graph. This means that the true temperature may not be exactly that found by adding the hot and cold junction temperatures. We will deal with this problem later, but it is not serious for heat treatment purposes.

The normal arrangement is that shown in Fig. 62. "A" is the hot junction and BB the wires within the immersed length – the materials being the "thermoelectric" alloy. CC are connecting wires leading to the meter "M" and "R" is a series resistance. If CC are plain copper conductors, then the effective cold junction will be at DD. This may be close to the furnace, and DD could be very hot. The effective cold junction can be moved to the meter either by using special alloy connecting cable (called a "compensating lead") or more simply by continuing the thermocouple element wire from A right through to M and R. This is the method I use; the meter need not be all that far away from the furnace, and one has to buy a yard or so of thermocouple wire anyway. The function of the resistance "R" is to reduce the effects of changes of resistance in the circuit which may occur

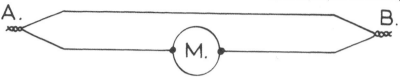

Fig. 61 *The principle of the thermocouple.*

as the couple element gets hot. If the resistance of BB and CC were, say 0.5 ohm and that of the meter 1.5 ohm, then any change in the former would be appreciable. By inserting this "ballast resistance" say 100 ohm, then the change in resistance of AA and CC with temperature will have negligible effect. It serves a further purpose, too. It can be used to match the indicator to the particular thermocouple used. We will make use of this when "adapting" instruments for homemade indicators.

THERMOCOUPLES

A number of different alloys are used for the thermocouple elements. The cheapest is copper against "Constantan" (60% Copper 40% Nickel) but this can operate safely only up to about 500°C. Chromel-Eureka (90% Ni 10% Cr vs 40% Ni 60% Cu) can be worked intermittently up to 850°C, or 700°C continuously, and has the merit that it delivers the highest EMF/ °C of any. Iron-Constantan is the next best in this respect, and can work continuously at 750°C and intermittently up to 1000°C. It is cheap, and well suited to our work, provided you recalibrate if it is used for long periods (days) above about 800°C. The commonest for high-temperature work is Chromel-Alumel (90% Ni 10% Cr vs 94% Ni, 2% Al + Si and Mn) which can work all day at 1200°C. It does not develop quite such a high EMF as the previous types, but sufficient for our purpose. There are other alloys, notably those based on Platinum, but none likely to be of interest to us. All these thermocouple alloys are now made to a British Standard Specification, and the following table, taken from "The Model Engineer's Handbook" shows the EMF developed in millivolts when the cold junction stands at 0°C. This assumes that the wire is to the relevant B.S., but the difference between this and others (e.g., to DIN std) is negligible.

The EMF in *Millivolts* developed by couples is given in the table.

A=Copper-Constantan to BS 1828
B=Iron-Constantan to BS 1829
C=NiChrome-NiAluminium BS 1827

$T°C$	A	B	C
0	0	0	0
50	2.20	2.58	2.02
100	4.24	5.27	4.10
150	6.63	8.01	6.13
200	9.18	10.78	8.13
250	11.86	13.56	10.16
300	14.67	16.33	12.21
350	17.58	19.09	14.29
400	20.59	21.85	16.40
500	26.10	27.39	20.65
600	—	33.11	24.91
700	—	39.15	29.14
800	—	45.53	33.30
900	—	—	37.4
1000	—	—	41.3
1200	—	—	48.9
1400	—	—	55.9

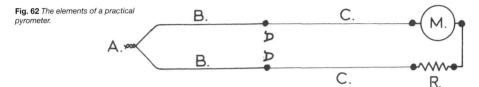

Fig. 62 *The elements of a practical pyrometer.*

Now, let us suppose that we are using an Iron-Constantan couple with the hot junction at 700°C and the cold at 100°C. The indicated voltage will be 39.15 − 5.27 = 33·88 mV. This corresponds to a temperature of 613°C. Add on the cold junction temperature and we find the sum to be 713°C − 13°C higher than it actually is. So, the cold junction must, first, be kept as cool as possible (in really accurate work it is set in ice in a thermos flask) and second, we should keep a thermometer nearby to check the temperature. If the cold junction is kept within +/− 2°C of 15°C, the error will not exceed two or three degrees if the cold junction temperature is simply added to that indicated on the meter. If the meter and thermocouple are CALIBRATED with the cold junction at 15°C the error will be negligible.

The construction of the thermocouple is simplicity itself. It can, indeed, work very satisfactorily if the wires are tightly twisted together. This will read correctly, but there will be a time-lag between reaching the temperature and that indicated. The ends can easily be welded together if you have a little Microflame oxy-butane torch or, indeed, any welding equipment. The gauge of wire is unimportant except as regards cost, and 26 gauge is very satisfactory, though I would prefer to see this in a protective sheath. That seen in Fig. 63 is 18 gauge, and this can be used in a furnace or even a salt pot with no sheath, though one is preferable in the latter case. Twin thermocouple pairs, about 30 gauge, insulated with fine heat-resistant sleeving, are available. For the knockabout work of heat treatment I would tend to favor the 18 gauge wire, but it IS only a question of fragility; there is no difference in the effectiveness.

The couple wires must, of course, be insulated behind the actual junction, and either single or twin bore ceramic or silica insulators can be had for this purpose from scientific instrument suppliers. (Griffin & George, Gallenkamp etc) or from Morgan Refractories, already mentioned in connection with muffles.

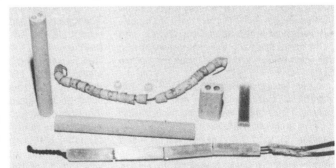

Fig. 63 *Foreground, a homemade thermocouple. The twisted end could be shorter with advantage. Center, various forms of twin wire couple insulators. Rear, single bead insulators for any form of wire in hot environments.*

Thermocouples and Pyrometers 109

Some of these are seen in Fig. 63. These may, in turn, be protected by setting the whole inside a steel sheath. The end can be closed either by folding over and hammering, or by welding in a plug. The sheath should be a fairly close fit on the insulators. This will protect the couple from knocks, and also (in the case of the salt pot) from a gradual eroding away of the wires. On the other hand, the sheath will cause a time-lag in the indications – your indicator will tend to read the temperature as it was 3 or 4 minutes earlier, depending on how heavy the tube is. There is no need, for our purposes, to use stainless steel. Once clear of the actual furnace the wires may be insulated with ordinary sleeving, or you can use the glass-fiber type if they are likely to get hot. Such sleeving can be obtained (or ordered) through radio service stores.

The Indicator. The maximum reading using iron-constantan will be about 50 millivolts, and for BS 1827 NiCr-NiAl, about 35 mV. If you have a "multimeter" with a millivolt scale, well and good; you can use this. Otherwise you must either buy one or make one. There was a time when "surplus" micro-ammeters were readily available, and these are of excellent quality. Those reading up to 50 or 100 μA would be the most suitable. But such meters are not expensive new and, again, can be ordered through radio service stores. A 0-50 meter will do nicely, but you must know its coil resistance, and if this is not stated in the catalog, obtain the information from the makers before buying it.

Now, let us suppose that we have the meter, 0-50μA, and its resistance is exactly 1000 ohm. We are home and dry, for one millivolt will give a deflection of 1 micro-amp, and the scale can be used directly. (The external resistance of the couple won't matter). Suppose, however,

that it is otherwise, and resistances of around 750 ohm are common. Let us suppose it is shown as 735 ohm. This is where the resistance "R" of Fig. 62 comes in. If we make this 1000 – 735 = 265 ohm, then we have a total resistance of 1000, and the meter will read directly. Such a resistance would be "built up" with one at 200, one at 50, and one at 15 ohm; again, from the radio service store, "High Stability 1% Tolerance" type.

However, suppose the meter has a resistance HIGHER than 1000 ohm, what then? I have one here, 0-100 μA, 1250 ohm. Apply Ohm's law. C = E/R, or, more conveniently, E = C × R. 100μA × 1250 Ω = 125,000 microvolts, or 125 millivolts. So, for a meter with a resistance "R" exceeding 1000 ohm, the conversion is "Actual Mv = Scale Mv × R/1000", where R is the meter resistance. It is as easy as that! Fig. 64 shows three meters, one circular "Ex Government" one, which is still as good as new; a small Japanese meter, really too small a scale length; and a large 0-100 meter which is, in fact, the one I would use despite its resistance of 1250 ohm.

Calibration. This is simply a check on the table, and ought to be done just in case the meter resistance is not as stated (they all are made to a tolerance) and after a period, in case there has been a change in the characteristics of the couple elements. The lower end is done at 100°C. The thermocouple is set in the steam above boiling water – NOT in the water itself. See Fig. 65, though it can be done in an electric kettle just as easily. Make sure that the cold junction (i.e. the meter, if used as in Fig. 62) is at 15°C. Let the junction soak for about ten minutes and observe the reading. Let it cool a little, and repeat. Do this three times and take the mean. For an intermediate temperature you can, if you have a tempering salt bath

110   HARDENING, TEMPERING, AND HEAT TREATMENT FOR HOME MACHINISTS

Fig. 64 Micro-ammeters.
Left 1½ in. square 0–50 µA, center, "Surplus" 0–100µA, right 4½ in. 0–100µA, normally used by the author.

and a mercury thermometer, use this. Strap the end of the couple to the thermometer bulb with care and a bit of thin wire and raise the temperature to some figure about the limit of the thermometer. Make sure the heater is stable, and take readings, three, with the temperature falling about 30°C and then raised again between each, and note the mean of the three.

For higher temperatures the following can be used. Lead, melting at 327°C, Zinc at 419°C (but be careful of the fumes) and pure aluminum (from an old saucepan) 658°C. In the case of the lead you will need a layer of resin on the surface to prevent oxidation, and may need to skim off oxide as well. The drill in this case is different. You bring the metal up *above* melting point and immerse the couple. Take away the heat, and start noting the temperature indicator every 30 seconds or so. As it cools you will find an "arrest point" developing (Fig. 66) and then as the metal is solid, the temperature falls again. Now reheat, and again note the temperatures – or the millivolts. Again

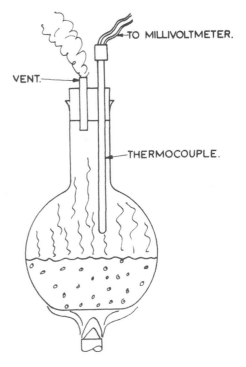

Fig. 65 One method of calibrating a thermocouple in steam. Any kind of container will do.

Thermocouples and Pyrometers   111

there will be an arrest in the INCREASE in temperature. Repeat this a couple of times, always removing any scum which forms on the surface of the metal. The mean of the arrest points is the actual melting point of the metal. You can do another at 801°C, with pure salt. Note, NOT the household variety. Ask at the chemists for "Sodium Chloride BPC" – this is common salt, but chemically pure.

Once all this has been done you can either make up a table or make a new scale out of paper to stick on the dial. I use a table, as I have other uses for microammeters and don't want to tie any of them up on one job.

The final alternative is expensive, but definitely "in the mood". You can buy (or some of you may be able to make, for all I know) a solid state digital indicator, which will read out the temperature on light-emitting diodes. If you have several thermocouples, high temperatures and low, you can build in to this a correcting circuit which will allow for the use of copper-constantan at one end of the temperature range and Platinum Rhodio-platinum at the other: a universal pyrometer indicator. This is not a book on electronics, so that I must leave the detail for you to sort out. Sufficient for most of the electronically minded to know that it can be done!

APPENDIX 2

Carbon Steel Cutting Tools

Many readers may never have made a cutting tool in their lives, apart from the odd D-bit, and would regard anything except high-speed steel (or even tungsten carbide) as being a very inferior tool indeed.

This is a mistake. The ONLY reason for using HSS is that it can operate at a higher temperature, and can, therefore, cut FASTER. HSS is much more expensive; it is not as hard as properly treated carbon tool-steel; at the proper cutting speed carbon steel has a longer tool life, and for finishing cuts below 80ft/min. lasts much longer. And (again, when properly treated) carbon steel will give a better finish. Nor is it true that "you can't take heavy cuts". This is nonsense. I have by me a table of "speeds and feeds" for carbon steel lathe tools which lists cuts up to one inch deep at feeds of one eighth of an inch per rev. Finally, carbon steel will tackle "the really hard stuff". Until very recently it was used for machining the chilled cast iron rolls used in steelworks (the surface deliberately made as hard as the hard spots you can't machine on your castings!) and watchmakers habitually cut hardened and tempered steel pivots with a carbon steel graver.

The *only* disadvantage which afflicts the material is that it "tempers" at quite a low figure. HSS is, initially, softer than carbon steel, (Fig, 66) but whereas the latter would start to lose some of its cutting hardness at about 270°C at the tool point the former can be operated so hot that the cutting oil will smoke and, indeed, I have seen special grades run for demonstration purposes cutting at a dull red heat. The same is true of Tungsten Carbide; its virtue is not its hardness – it is intended as a FAST CUTTING TOOL, perhaps at three times the speed of HSS.

This is the crux of the matter. You can buy a couple of feet of carbon tool steel for the price of one short HSS toolbit; you can file it, bend it, forge it, and harden it to cut tough alloy steel, even hard cast iron; and you can get superb tool finish on the work. But you MUST keep the cutting speed down and keep the tool point cool. For roughing cuts the speed should be about one third that used for HSS (though if the coolant supply is good you can try faster) and for normal finishing cuts the machine should be run at about two thirds that used for HSS. In fact, for brass or free-cutting mild steel, taking model engineers' finishing cuts, there may be no

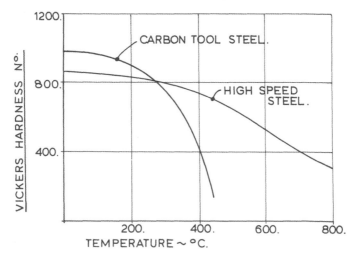

Fig. 66 *The effect of working temperature on the hardness of typical carbon and high-speed tool-steel. Once the tool reaches a particular temperature the former hardness will not be restored on cooling. Note that carbon steel has the advantage if the tip temperature can be kept below about 250°C.*

need to reduce speed at all. (I am, of course, assuming that you use the "proper" HSS cutting speeds; many model engineers run at carbon steel speeds all the time!) Carbon steel will cut anything that can be cut by HSS, and many that we often use carbide for (and doesn't chip at the edges either) but it does take longer. But what is the hurry, anyway?

On the question of "quality of finish" it is not always appreciated that the surface of the workpiece is, when taking very fine cuts, a reflection of the surface of the tool. If the tool point has grooves from the grinder it must leave grooves or ribs on the work. Carbon steel has a finer grain than most HSS, and if grain refined, even more so. Properly hardened, and tempered only so far as is essential, it takes up a better finish from the oilstone, thus giving an even better finish to the work. In "Ornamental Turning" we have to go further still; we rely entirely on the "tool finish" for the decorative reflective surfaces which are so much admired, and even go to the length of lapping the cutting edge with rouge on an iron lap!

With the ever-increasing cost of all alloy steels (and HSS in particular) it does make some sense to reconsider the place of the "old fashioned" carbon steel. We are not all that concerned with optimum floor-to-floor times, and few of us would ever consider working our tools as hard as they do in industry. (The "economic tool life" may be no more than 42 minutes on center-lathe work!). I would not, of course, suggest that we abandon HSS wholesale; that would be foolish. But for what it is worth I will conclude this note by observing that ALL the crankshafts I have made, and that is quite a lot, have been finished, and most of them roughed, using carbon steel tools on the crankpins, and most have been turned on the journals that way as well. Why not give it a trial?

APPENDIX 3

British Standard Steel Specification Numbers

The Old British Standard 970/1955, characterized by the "EN" numbers which many of us still use, was replaced by the new BS970 in 1972. It really is time that we started to use it! It has one great advantage, in that the BS number itself gives us the carbon content for many steels.

The number comprises three digits, followed by a letter, followed by two more digits. The first three digits serve two purposes. They give a broad indication of the TYPE of steel; thus –

000 to 199 are all "plain" carbon steel with some manganese content

200 to 240 are "Free-cutting" versions of the above

300 to 499 are all "Stainless" or "Heat Resisting" steels

500 to 999 are all "Alloy" steels and within the number the main alloying elements can be identified.

We are concerned (for heat treatment) only with the plain carbon steels and, perhaps, their free-cutting equivalent. The first digit can be ignored; 0 and 1 mean "plain" and 2 means "free-cutting". The second two digits, (preceded by 0 or 1) give the manganese content multiplied by 100; thus 145 means 0.45% manganese. If preceded by 2, these digits indicate the

sulfur content, again, × 100. So, 224 will be a 0.24% sulfur steel.

The second group of two digits indicates the carbon content multiplied by 100. Thus 45 indicates a 0.45% carbon steel. The letter shows the basis of the specification. "M" means that the steel must meet the mechanical properties of the material; "A" means that it must be to the specified chemical analysis, other properties being secondary; "H" means that it must meet the requirements of Hardenability. Most of the steel we use is to the "M" specification.

There is, of course, a tolerance on the % figures for carbon and other materials; thus 0.2% carbon may lie between 0.16 and 0.24% – though the user can (provided he pays) specify closer limits.

As a general rule, therefore, *approximate* heat treatment procedures can be deduced from the specification number. Thus 080M30 is a 0.3% carbon 0.8% manganese steel, which may be heat treated by quenching from about 875°C and tempering to suit the application. We can also deduce from the iron-carbon diagram on page 18 that it should be normalized at around 880°C.

The specification does not cover "Tool Steels", with more than 1% carbon.

APPENDIX 4

Approximate Conversion of Hardness Scales (ASTM Conversion Tables)

SHORE No.	VICKERS VDP	ROCKWELL "C"	(For Steels) UTS 1000 Lbf/Sq.in.
99	1030	70	
98	970	69	–
97	940	68	–
95	900	67	–
93	880	66.4	–
91	840	65.3	–
90	820	64.7	–
88	800	64	–
86	760	62.5	–
84	740	61.6	–
82	710	60.5	–
80	680	59.2	330
78	650	57.8	314
76	630	56.8	304
74	600	55.2	289
72	580	54.1	280
70	550	52.3	264
68	530	51.1	254
66	500	49.1	240
64	480	47.7	230

SHORE No.	VICKERS VDP	ROCKWELL "C"	(For Steels) UTS 1000 Lbf/Sq.in.
62	460	46.1	220
60	446	45	213
58	430	43.6	204
56	410	41.8	195
54	396	40.2	194
52	380	38.8	180
50	360	36.6	170
48	354	34.9	163
46	330	33.3	156
44	314	31.4	148
42	300	29.8	141
40	280	27.1	131
38	270	25.6	126
36	250	22.2	116
34	240	20.3	111
32	220	15.7(95B)	101
30	210	13.4(93.4B)	97
28	190	8.5(89.5B)	88
26	180	6.0(87.1B)	84
24	160	0 (81.7B)	75
22	150	(78.7B)	71
20	130	(71.2B)	62
18	122	(67.6B)	58

Rockwell "C" is not applicable below this range. Rockwell "B" in brackets

These conversions must be used with discretion, especially as regards the Ultimate Tensile Strength column. They relate only to Carbon and low alloy steel, and exclude "Stainless" steels.

Approximate Conversion of Hardness Scales (ASTM Conversion Tables)

Glossary of Terms

A.I.S.I	American Iron and Steel Institute.
A.S.M.E.	American Society of Mechanical Engineers
A.S.T.M.	American Society for Testing Materials
Acicular	Crystals forming a needle-like structure in place of the more usual grains.
Alloy Steel	Steel containing elements other than iron and carbon, though up to 0.35% Manganese is found in all steels.
Annealing	A heat treatment which softens an already hardened steel.
Arrest point	Points at which the temperature ceases to rise for a short period when the steel is heated slowly, and similarly when cooling.
Austempering	A constant temperature transformation process, mainly used for small parts, springs, etc. Fig. 44.
Austenite	A solid solution of carbon in iron.
B.S.I.	British Standards Institution.
Bainite	A structure obtained when Austenite is transformed at a constant low temperature, less hard, but tougher than Martensite. Typically the result of "Austempering".
Billet	A square or rectangular bar, usually the raw material for later hot forming processes.
Blister Steel	The name given to the steel after the completion of the cementation process. The surface of the metal is at this point covered in scale blisters.
Body Centered	Applied to crystals, one with an atom at each corner and one in the geometric center of the lattice.
Brine	Concentrated solution of common salt (NaCl) in water.
Carburise	Any process which causes absorption of carbon.
Caseharden	A surface hardening process which retains the normal structure of the steel in the core of the part. Normally achieved by surface carburising, heating, and quenching.
Cast Steel	The name given to high-carbon steel which has been melted after the cementation process is complete. At one time synonymous with tool-steel it is now liable to be confused with castings made from "mild" steel. The terms "Crucible Steel" or "High Carbon Steel" are to be preferred.

Cementation	The process by which Wrought Iron is caused to absorb carbon through the full thickness of the metal, to produce "Blister" or "High Carbon" steel.
Cementite	Metallurgical name for Iron Carbide, Fe_3C. So named because it was first identified in steel made by cementation.
Critical Temperature	The temperature at which structural changes occur in the metal. Usually, but not always, coincident with the "Arrest Points".
Crystal	An orderly arrangement of atoms, almost always in precise geometric shapes. Iron crystals are always of cubic form.
Curie Point	The temperature above which steel loses its magnetic properties, around 770°C.
Dannemorra	An ironworks in Sweden, which was reputed to produce an iron remarkably free from impurities.
Decarburise	The reduction of carbon content, usually on the surface of the metal. Caused as a rule by the action of oxygen or iron oxides at high temperatures.
EN No.	The "Engineering Number", the identification number of steels used in B.S.970/1955, now superseded.
Equilibrium Diagram	A chart plotting the critical temperatures of steel against the carbon content. Fig. 13.
Eutectoid	The composition of steel at which the upper critical temperature coincides with the lower. "Eutectoid" steel is entirely pearlitic.
Face Centered	Applied to crystals, one with an atom at each corner and one in the center of each of the faces of the lattice.
Faggoting	The act of welding together bars of Wrought Iron to make billets.
Ferrite	Metallurgical name for the almost pure iron observed in the microstructure of steel. (Not to be confused with the "sintered ferrite" used for coil cores etc in electronic equipment.)
Gauge Stock	An oil-hardening carbon-chromium alloy steel compounded to reduce distortion on quenching to a minimum. Sometimes known as "ground flat stock".
Grain	Aggregates of crystals. These form when the metal solidifies, but may change their shape and disposition as it cools.
Grain Refinement	Any process which either reduces or makes more uniform the size of the grains.

Glossary of Terms   119

High Carbon Steel	Steel with a carbon content above 0.85%. More accurately, steel which shows free Cementite in the microstructure.
High-speed steel	Usually a high-Chromium high-Tungsten alloy with enhanced hot-hardness, but may not be a steel at all. "Stellite" is an alloy of Cobalt, Chromium and Tungsten, with no Iron content.
IZOD number	The energy in foot-pounds required to break a standard specimen under a prescribed impact load. A test for shock resistance.
Lattice	A framework of imaginary lines joining the location of atoms in a crystal.
Liquidus	The temperature above which the metal is entirely liquid.
Martempering	Heat treatment process designed to reduce distortion on large or complex components. Fig. 45.
Martensite	The structure formed when a combination of Austenite and Cementite is cooled too quickly to allow the normal transformation to Pearlite.
Melting Range	The range of temperature between the Solidus and the Liquidus, where the metal is in a pasty state, with both solid and liquid present.
Muffle	A furnace in which the work is protected from the direct impingement of the heating flame. It is now applied also to most electric resistance furnaces.
Neutral Salt	A salt which is used as a heating medium but which neither carburises nor decarburises the metal.
Nodular	A condition where the Iron Carbide grains are in the form of nodules rather than the normal needle-like shape.
Normalize	Heat treatment intended to restore distorted grains to their normal shape. A form of grain refinement.
O.H. & T.	Oil hardened and Tempered.
Pearlite	The normal transformation product when Austenite is slowly cooled through the lower critical temperature. It consists of sub-microscopic "plates" or laminae of Ferrite and Cementite.
Puddling	The process of converting cast iron into wrought iron.
RN(c)	Rockwell Hardness test number, on the "c" scale, the one normally used for hard materials.
Recalescence	The name sometimes used for the critical temperatures.

S.A.E.	Society for Automotive Engineers (USA).
"S" Curve	Curve showing transformation rates against temperature and time. (Fig. 16).
Scale	Iron Oxide forming on the surface of hot steel.
Solid Solution	The condition where the atoms of one solid substance are disposed within the crystal lattice of another. Analagous to the more usual liquid solution.
Solidus	Temperature below which the metal is entirely solid.
Steel	Iron-carbon alloy with a carbon content between 0.01% and 1.7%. Before about 1855 the term was universally applied only to "High Carbon Steel" as we know it.
Silver Steel	High Carbon Steel to BS.1407. So-called because it is usually ground and so presents a "silvery" appearance, in contrast to the normal "black" tool steel of earlier days. Typically 1.1-1.2% Carbon, 0.3-0.4% Managanese, 0.4-0.5% Chromium, 0.1-0.25% Silicon, and maxima of 0.35% Sulfur & Phosphorus.
Tempering	A reheating process which modifies the structure of a heat-treated steel. (Note that in early books the "Temper" of a steel often referred to its carbon content).
T.T.T. Curve	"Time-Temperature Transformation Curve – the "S" Curve of Fig. 16. A chart which shows the time taken for constant temperature transformation of steel.
Transformation	Any change of the microscopic structure or chemical composition of steel brought about by heat treatment.
U.T.S.	Ultimate Tensile Strength. The stress at the breaking point, measured under prescribed conditions on a standard test piece.
V.D.P.	Vickers Diamond Pyramid. The VDP number is a measure of the hardness of the material.
Wrought Iron	The predecessor to steel. Made by decarburising cast iron in the puddling furnace.
Yield Point	The stress beyond which metal will not return to its original length when the load is removed.

Glossary of Terms

Index

See also the glossary on page 118 for definitions of terms used.

Acicular grains, 21, 118
Air/gas torches, 54
Alloy steels, 25
Annealing, 71
Arrest point, 14, 118
A.S.M.E., 118
Austempering, 79
Austenite, 16
Austenising temperature, 28, 29, 30, 33

Bainite, 118
Bench, heat treatment, 102
Bessemer Steel, 11
"Best" wroughtiron, 10
Blacksmiths hearth, 51
Blastfurance, 7
Blazing off, 49
Blister Steel, 118
Blowlamps, 53
Blowlamps flame, 54
"Blueing steel, 81
Body center crystal, 14
Bricks, 56
Bricks, heating, 99
Brine, proportions, 32
Brinell test, 84, 116
British Standard Steel specification, 115
Burns, from hot salt, 105
    treatment, 105

Carburising   64, 67Case hardening, 64
Cast Steel, 11
Cementation, 11
Cementite, 17, 119

Clothing, protective, 103
Coil springs, 77
Cold junction, 107
Cooling rates, 20
Constantan, 108
Control systems, furnace, 61
Cosmetic heat treatment, 81
Critical temperature, 19
Crucible steel, 11
Crystals, 13
Curie point, 15
Cutting speed, carbon steel, 113
Dannemorra, 119
Decarburising, 37
Die quenching, 57
Die tempering, 49
Distortion, 23
Domestic fire heating, 51

Electrical safety, 106
EMF of thermocouples, 108
"E.N" number, 120
Energy controller, 61
Equilibrium diagram, 19
Eutectoid steel, 19, 120

Face center crystal, 14
Faggoting, 10
Ferrite, 7, 17, 119
File steel, 29
File test, hardness, 89
Fire extinguisher, 103
Fire risks, 102
Forging, 82

122 HARDENING, TEMPERING, AND HEAT TREATMENT FOR HOME MACHINISTS

Frothing (of salt bath), 104
FURNACES.
  Blast, 7
  Electric, 59
  Gas fired, 57
  Muffle, gas, 90
  Muffle, home made, 94
  Puddling, 10
  Radiant, 93
  Salt, high temperature, 98

Gas furnace, 57, 90
Gas torches, 54
Gauge stock, 24, 120
Goggles, 103, 104
Grains, 14, 119
Grain refining (carburising), 74
Ground Gauge Stock, 24

Hardness comparison, chart, 116
Hardness comparison HSS and tool-
  steel, 114
Heat testing, 84
Heat pipe, 48
Heat treatment for toughness, 75
Heating time, 28
High-speed steel, 72, 82, 120
Homemade muffles, 90
Hot junction (thermocouple), 107
Huntsman progress, 11

Insulating bricks, 56
Insulating wool, 98
Insulators, thermocouple, 109
Iron, 7
  -carbide, 17
  Pig, 8
  Wrought, 9
Iron-carbon equilibrium diagram, 19
IZOD number, 120

Kasenit process, 67
Kiln, gas-fired, 58

Lathe tools, carbon steel, 113
  tempering, 43, 74
Liquidus, 121

Martempering, 79, 120
Martensite, 21, 120
Millivoltmeter, 109
MOH's hardness scale, 84
Muffle – Electric, 59
  Gas fired, 57
  Home made, 90, 94

Neutral salts, 121
Nicherome wire, 108
Normalising, 72, 120

Open fire heating, 51
"Ornamental Turning" tools, 74
Overheating, 37
Oxy-acetylene, 53

Paraffin blowlamp, 55
Pearlite, 17, 120
Propane torch, 55
"Puddling, 120
Pyrometers, 107

Quenching, in brine, 31
  in oil, 32, 38
  in water, 31
Quenching techniques, 38-40

Radiant element furnace, 93
Recalescence, 120
Rehardening, 73
Resistance wire, 101
Rockwell hardness test, 85, 116
Rototherm thermometer, 107

S.A.E., 121
S-curve, 21
Salt bath, Austenising, 60, 98
  Safety, 104
  Tempering, 45

Index 123

Scaling, 31, 73
Scleroscope, 86
Seegar Cones, 31
Shore hardness test, 86, 116
Silver steel, 25
  Annealing, 71
  Austenising temperature, 29
  Specification, 121
  Tempering, 42
Slag, 8
Solid Solution, 15
Solidus, 121
Spirit lamp, 47, 62
Springs, 24, 77, 79
Steel, Alloy, 25
  Carbon, 12
  Casehardening, 68
  Cast or Crucible, 11
  File, 29
  Medium carbon, 75
  Hardness and Toughness, 20
  Mild, 11
Stress relieving, 72
Surface hardening, 64

Temperature,
  Annealing, 71
  Austenising, 29
  Colors (plates), 33
  Holding times, 28, 44
  Indicator crayons, 30
  Judging, 29
  Normalising, 72
  Stress relieving, 72
  Tempering see below.
Tempering, 24, 41, 50
  Colors, 36, 43, 47
  Lathe tools, 43
  Tools, various, 42
  Time, 44

Themocouples, 107, 110
Thermostat control, 61
Through hardening, 23
Time-Temperture transformation, 22
Tongs, 62
Tool materials, 27
Torches, 53
Torch flame temperature, 54
Transformation diagrams, 18, 21
Tube furnace, 58, 90

U,T.S., 121

Vickers Hardness Test (VDP), 86, 116

Wire, electric heating, 101
  thermocouple, 108

Yield Point, 123

LIST OF TABLES

Carbon context of tool steels, 27
Color & Temperature,
  700-1000°C, 30
  215-330°C, 43
Hardness. Comparison of scales, 116
  Typical values, 88
Temperatures.
  Annealing, 71
  Austenising, 29
  Celsius to Fahrenheit, 125, 126
  Grain refining, 67
  Normalising, 72
  Oven, domestic, 45
  Quenching, 29
  Tempering, 42
Thermocouple wire, EMF, 108

Temperatures	
Celcius	Fahrenheit
0	32
10	50
15	59
20	68
30	86
50	122
60	140
70	158
100	212
120	248
140	284
150	302
160	320
170	338
180	356
190	374
195	383
200	392
204	400
210	410
215	419
220	428
225	437
230	446
235	455
240	464
245	473

Temperatures	
Celcius	Fahrenheit
250	482
255	491
260	500
265	509
270	518
275	527
280	536
285	545
290	554
295	563
300	572
305	581
310	590
315	599
320	608
325	617
327	621
330	626
360	680
400	752
419	786
420	788
427	800
500	932
538	1000
550	1022
600	1112

Temperatures	
Celcius	Fahrenheit
613	1135
649	1200
650	1202
658	1216
670	1238
700	1292
704	1300
713	1315
720	1328
725	1337
730	1346
735	1355
750	1382
760	1400
770	1418
780	1436
790	1454
800	1472
801	1474
816	1500
820	1508
825	1517
830	1526
840	1544
850	1562
860	1580

Temperatures	
Celcius	Fahrenheit
870	1598
875	1607
880	1616
890	1634
899	1650
900	1652
910	1670
920	1688
925	1697
950	1742
982	1800
1000	1832
1050	1922
1100	2012
1130	2066
1150	2102
1200	2192
1250	2282
1300	2372
1392	2538
1400	2552
1427	2600
1430	2606
1500	2732
1600	2912